POCKET
LAW

POCKET
LAW

TONY WALES

THE ECONOMIST IN ASSOCIATION WITH
PROFILE BOOKS LTD

Profile Books Ltd, Registered Office:
62 Queen Anne Street, London W1M 9LA

First published by Profile Books Ltd
in association with
The Economist Newspaper Ltd 1997

Printed by
LEGO S.p.a. - Vicenza - Italy

A CIP catalogue record for this book is available
from the British Library

ISBN 1 86197 008 0

CONTENTS

INTRODUCTION

This is not a comprehensive legal textbook. If it was, it would not fit in your pocket.

Its aims are to pull back some of the veils of confusion over the law, to remove some of the mystique that surrounds it, to explode some of the jargon that lawyers use and to give a better insight into basic legal principles in areas where businessmen and managers have to operate. At their root these principles are not complicated, and they largely (but not always) accord with common sense, but after years of manipulation by clever lawyers, common sense can be hard to find.

Lawyers are paid to find tortuous interpretations of seemingly straightforward concepts. Their clients' interests depend on their skill to do so, and sometimes black can be explained away as white. Also, because inevitably there is another lawyer on the other side seeking to stretch the interpretation in the opposite direction, the judicial meaning is often a balance between competing arguments, rather than a clear-cut position. This produces grey areas, not pristine black or white, which can be exploited next time by another clever lawyer, thereby adding another colour to the mixture. As every five-year-old knows, at least after some experiment in art class, if you mix too many colours all you get is a deep shade of murky brown. Add another colour and it just gets deeper and murkier. So the law, by the nature of the system, looks deep and murky. This book cannot separate the colours, but it should help you to recognise the existence of a mixture.

One focus of the book is legal jargon. In any industry the players give names to familiar ideas so that they can refer to them in a form of short-hand. Abbreviations and metaphors are fun. They add a little spice to otherwise boring ideas. Unfortunately, the law is prone to boring ideas. Also, as it is intrinsically bound up with language, it is prone to linguistic acrobatics. Worse, because lawyers tend to be pompous (a gross and unfair generalisation, of course), the law is prone to pompous linguistic jargon. There is a suspicion that lawyers use obscure language, particularly jargon, deliberately (or perhaps subconsciously) to add a mystique to the law. If they let their clients have too clear an insight into the system, the clients may not need to pay for their translation services. Like medieval alchemists, some lawyers see themselves as keepers of magic spells. These spells must be treated with extreme care, lest they fall into uneducated hands, and must be dispensed sparingly – and for hefty sums of money. If the spells become common knowledge, they are devalued. It is better to shroud them in mists of wonder and keep a firm grip on them.

Another feature of *Pocket Law* is an attempt to cross some borders. Laws are intrinsically bound to the jurisdiction that spawned them. One country's system will be significantly different from its neighbour's, even where they have a common root. The US legal system is founded on and shares a common language with the English system, but it has developed on its own and is now far removed. Similarly, Commonwealth countries have put their own interpretation on English law and have made notable diversions from it. The civil law systems of continental Europe started from a radically different standpoint and continue to move further away, regardless of the attempts of the European Union to push them together. However, despite all the evidence of separation and division, different legal systems can have remarkably similar principles. Further, even when they opt for diametrically opposed principles, it is still possible to understand (from the viewpoint of the other, competing jurisdiction) how that conclusion was reached. All of this helps with an understanding of the law and how lawyers work.

I should like to thank the following: my fellow commuters on the morning train from Guildford via Cobham to London Waterloo for giving me some uninterrupted time each day for pondering and occasional scribbling; Helen Theophanous and Katie Mawdsley for putting an untidy manuscript into tidy order and Geoffrey Reed of Browne Jacobson for correcting some of the more obvious errors; Stephen Brough for his guidance and encouragement; and *The Economist* for being the type of institution to encourage a work like this.

Tony Wales

Part 1
ESSAYS

How to use lawyers

Like colonic irrigation, lawyers are an uncomfortable means to a desirable end. Unfortunately, unlike colonic irrigation, you do not have much choice but to use them. They are, in truth, a necessity. You are unwise if you think you can sell your house, make your will, ply your trade, manage your business or enter into any significant contract without checking your legal position. If you do not take legal advice, you are at risk. You cannot assume that your common sense will carry you through the legal minefield unscathed. It is a dangerous world out there.

The problems with using lawyers are well known. Most are expensive; many are bad communicators; some are not competent (or, at least, not competent in all the fields in which they consider themselves to be experts); some are insufferably self-important; and a few are hopelessly uncommercial. The same problems, or course, can be attributed to many professional advisers. Like auditors and others, lawyers are seen as a burden – albeit a necessary burden – to a smooth-running business. But it does not have to be this way, and your own attitude and approach can have an important impact on your relationship with your lawyer. You can help your lawyer to help you; you can certainly help your lawyer be more efficient and effective.

Here are a few golden rules.

Good preparation. You should have a clear idea of what you are trying to achieve. You do not want to pay your lawyer for helping to get your own thoughts in order.

Get a free start. A common bleat from lawyers is that their clients do not consult them early enough; this is not surprising, since the client fears the taxi meter will start running earlier than necessary. This can be avoided by a direct, and honest, request for some free guidance at an early stage, perhaps before the deal has been finalised.

If you explain the possibilities to your lawyer, it is more than likely that he or she will give you a free preliminary consultation to make sure you are on the right legal track. If the deal goes ahead, the lawyer will get the formal instructions. If it does not, he has not lost much and has cemented a client relationship. All of this depends, of course, on your relationship with a lawyer; you have to feel comfortable about making that important request for a free hour or so.

Do not go too early. If you irritate your lawyer with requests for mere hand-holding, rather than useful action, you will be penalised by the ticking meter. You should give firm instructions only when you have a firm deal. The lawyer's job should be to document the commercial agreement you have made, with a bit of leveraging on your side when it comes to the technical issues. If you expect your lawyer to do more, you are not up to your own job.

Set a timetable. Any commercial arrangement should be based on a realistic timetable for its implementation. Without it the lawyers will dictate their own pace, which might allow them to clock up too many hours. The shorter the timetable, the less time there is for clock-running.

Pick the right lawyer. There are "horses for courses". It is no good consulting your trusted real-estate lawyer for a cross-border distribution agreement. Similarly, you should not assume that your excellent tax lawyer has a corporate partner who can deliver the same speed and quality of advice. Reputation goes a long way, so ask around; but there is no substitute for testing someone on the way he works with you. Give him a chance on a small job first; if it works well, go on to bigger jobs. If you are really in the dark or it is a new area for you, get several firms to make a presentation of their skills in a beauty parade and choose the one that seems most suited to your needs.

Agree fees at the beginning. It is no good hoping you can press for a good deal on fees after you have made your lawyer work every weekend for a month. It has got to be done at the beginning. Most lawyers these days are open to a discussion on fees. Ask for an estimate. Talk about a fixed fee, or at least a cap, to limit your exposure. If you send a lot of work, ask for a volume discount.

Agree the extent of the team. Some law firms make extra money by loading a job with swarms of lawyers, perhaps by bringing in experts (for tax, planning, cross-border work and so on) or teams of juniors (beware of trainees learning at your cost). You should identify and limit the required team at the beginning. You should not pay for anyone you have not approved as part of the team.

Maintain close communication. It is no good assuming your lawyer knows what you want. You have to stay in touch throughout the project, discussing developments, testing ideas, reviewing options. If you do not make your thoughts known, you cannot complain if your lawyer proceeds on assumptions.

Listen to advice. If you have chosen well, your lawyer will probably have more experience than you in the implementation of your specific project. So ask for advice and listen to the reply. It does not mean you should necessarily follow it, but you should get advice on all the available options (and the relevant consequences of each one) before deciding what to do. If it is a difficult decision, ask for the advice in writing so you can mull it over.

Do not be afraid to complain. If you are unhappy with the way things are going, say so. Your lawyer cannot be expected to put things right if you do not tell him they have gone wrong. These days even lawyers are aware of the importance of client service, so most will be open to your feedback.

None of these ideas, by itself, will make life with your lawyer easy, but a combination of some of them should save you from a truly bad experience. A continuing relationship with your lawyer should also help, as each of you will begin to understand the idiosyncrasies of the other. Eventually, this will nurture an established bond of trust between lawyer and client, which is powerful, but it can only grow with time, experience and luck.

How to Write a Contract

Your lawyer will tell you not to tread on sacred ground for fear of the sky falling on your head, but there is no reason why those in business should not compose their own contracts. Of course, you have to be aware of and follow some legal rules, but they are not impossible to grasp. Knowledge of your industry and its particular practices should also put you in a good position to deal with the pertinent issues.

In deciding whether you should have a go yourself or phone your lawyer depends on many things, such as the availability of your time, your confidence in putting pen to paper succinctly and your understanding of the basic rules. Probably the most important factor is risk. If the contract involves a potentially high liability for you, it is worth spending some money on getting it right. You do not want to bet the farm on your own legal expertise unless you are a legal expert. However, if your maximum exposure is £1,000, it is not worth paying £2,000 to your lawyer for drawing up the contract. Similarly, if you use a particular contract regularly, you might want a lawyer to approve the basic, standard form which you can then adapt for individual circumstances. It is worth paying the legal fees to put you on the right track at the beginning, with periodic reviews to make sure you are up-to-date.

Although this is nothing like an exhaustive list of all the legal rules, here are a few ideas that should be considered in writing a contract or in reading one before you sign it.

Parties. Think about who is doing what to whom. You have to include everyone who is going to perform an obligation and everyone for whose benefit the obligations will be performed. The rule of privity of contract says that, to be able to enforce the terms of a contract, you have got to be a party to it.

Names. You must get the names right. If a party

is a company, you have to spell out the exact company name, right down to Limited (or Ltd). If you do not, the individual who signs on behalf of the company may become personally liable under the contract.

Date. Many people, even lawyers, get hung up about the correct date to put on a contract, particularly where the terms of the contact are already in effect when the parties come to sign. A golden rule is never to backdate. The contract should be dated with the date on which the parties sign (or the date of the last to sign). If their obligations have already commenced, and the contract is intended to record this, you should insert a definition such as "the effective date" (which will be a date earlier, or later, if the circumstances require, than the date of signature) and make the terms of the contract effective from that date.

Consideration. Unless it is a deed (that is, a contract signed under seal), it must have consideration to make it a binding contract. In crude terms, consideration means doing something or promising to do something for someone else. In a contract everybody has to give consideration to everybody else. Usually, it is self-evident. One party delivers goods or services to the other; the other pays for them. Or each party makes a promise to the other; this is good consideration. Difficulties arise only when you find that all the obligations are being carried out by one party. If the other is not required to do anything at all, you have to invent some nominal consideration to make the contract enforceable. This is why you see strange provisions in contracts such as "For a consideration of £1" or "In return for a peppercorn, if demanded". These are merely techniques to inject the necessary element of consideration.

Definitions. If you define a few terms at the beginning of the contract, they act as abbreviations throughout the document and can allow you to be more succinct. There is no point, however, in using definitions unless you are going to refer to them several times. There is nothing more irritating in reading a contract than finding a solitary expression with capitalised first letters (thereby suggesting it is a defined term) and having to plough through pages of definitions to find out what it means.

Termination. No contract lasts for ever (although some, once completed, no longer have any effect), so you have to consider the termination provisions. These are vital in the case of a continuing relationship, such as a distribution agreement, which will have to be brought to an end at some time. The obvious provision is to allow either party to terminate on giving an agreed period of notice, but you may also want to provide for immediate termination in the event of default by the other party, insolvency or other specified circumstances. You should also deal with the consequences of termination, such as the return of each party's property or compensation payments.

Tax. Every contractual relationship should be reviewed from a tax viewpoint. The issue may merely be whether the seller should collect sales tax or value-added tax from the buyer, but there may be a wider issue concerning income tax or corporation tax that might have a bearing on how the contract should be drafted.

Title and risk. If the contract needs to pass ownership in goods or any property, you should think carefully about title and risk, then provide for the transfer of each at the appropriate time. You should draw a clear picture of who transfers ownership of what to whom, and when. Title equates to ownership. This is often the very substance of a contract, but there can be confusion as to when title actually transfers. The problem is apparent in a distribution agreement, where ownership has to pass from the manufacturer or supplier to the distributor and then to the customer. The timing of each transfer may be crucial. Risk is another issue. In simple terms, your risk is your responsibility for the property transferred. Risk does not necessarily pass at the same time as title. If you sign a conditional contract for the acquisition of property, risk will probably transfer on signature (and exchange) of contracts, but title passes only when the conditions have been fulfilled and the contract is completed (closed, in US jargon). The parties should agree on the appropriate time to transfer title and risk; the contract should reflect their agreement.

Payment. Price is inevitably important, and you should not leave any room for confusion. Make sure you remember to deal with sales tax or value-added tax. Are there any deductions? Are there any variables? Is there a currency exchange risk? It may be advisable to define the pricing formula so the correct price can be calculated whatever happens. The terms of payment are also important and are easily overlooked. One party may assume it will make payment on its normal terms of business, say, at the end of the month following receipt of the invoice. The other may expect payment within seven days of the date of the invoice. They should sort this out and put it in the contract.

Intellectual property. In most commercial contracts these days there is some element of intellectual property. Every business has a trade mark or a trade name or, at least, some reputation to protect. The transfer of goods usually entails one of these elements attaching to the goods, but the seller will not usually expect the buyer to acquire any rights over it. The contract should dictate who owns the intellectual property rights and the limited licence, if any, for other parties to make use of them.

Succinct drafting. Keep it simple. If the language is not readily understood by an ordinary person, there is a danger that a judge also will not understand it. Do not try to tackle too many issues in a single clause; divide them logically into separate provisions and separate clauses. Keep sentences short and to the point. Avoid adjectives. Pare down the words to their simplest meaning. Do not meander or waffle. Think it through carefully; write it down clearly.

None of these ideas, by itself, will produce an effective (or even enforceable) contract, but a combination of all of them may just do the trick. Drafting needs some thought and, if hurried, is likely to be flawed. You have to make sure you cover all the relevant issues – omission of one vital ingredient may wreck the whole picture – but similarly you must avoid irrelevancies. Before you cross the road stop, look and listen; then proceed confidently but cautiously to the other side.

How to set up a business in another country

Some countries go out of their way to attract incoming investment, offering tax breaks and other incentives for newcomers; others see it as less of a priority and are accused of frightening foreigners away with penal tax treatment or unfathomable bureaucracy. From the stony-faced immigration officer to the suspicious tax inspector, there are needless discomforts to endure, but on the whole the world is moving towards more cross-border investment. Anyone who tried to open a bank account in Prague first in 1985 and then in 1995 will see obvious progress.

It is easier to operate in some places than in others and every jurisdiction has its own local rules, which have to be checked carefully. There are a number of principles, however, that generally apply when someone sets up a business presence in another country. Here are some ideas to consider.

Representative office. The toe-in-the-water approach is to establish a minimal presence with a representative office. This is an informal arrangement which usually avoids registration with the regulatory authorities (or only minimal registration without much of a burden) and, more importantly, should not expose you to local tax on the profits of your business. To qualify for this lowly status, you will probably have to demonstrate that your activities are merely supporting operations for your main business, which is conducted outside the territory. These might be information-gathering or marketing activities, but not any significant trading operations. For example, if the local office customarily enters into trading contracts on its own account, it cannot claim it is merely a representative office. If it operates as a profit centre, it will have to pay tax on those profits, but there are many good reasons why a business will want to set up a service operation or similar activity which falls short of a profit centre.

Branch office. This is the level above a representative office, where your business presence amounts to a fully fledged trading activity, but it is nevertheless an extension of your head-office operations. A branch office shares the same legal identity as your head office; it does not have any separate legal personality and is governed by the same constitution. A branch is usually required to be registered with the local regulatory and tax authorities (with a view to paying tax on profits arising from its local operations). The regulatory regime will typically require you to file details of your head office entity (if it is a company, its by-laws or memorandum and articles of association and perhaps its annual accounts) and a named person residing in the local jurisdiction who is authorised to accept service of process on behalf of the branch.

Foreign subsidiary. This is the final frontier – going all the way. Establishing a foreign subsidiary is creating a new legal entity in the local jurisdiction. It will be formed under and governed by the laws of that jurisdiction. You may own its shares and control its management, but otherwise it is the same as any other local corporation. It can sue and be sued in its own name. It pays the same taxes as other local companies and is governed by the same regulatory regime.

Taxation. One issue you should always check is the local tax treatment. Benign authorities, such as Hong Kong, seek only to tax profits arising from a source within their jurisdiction, so profits earned in Singapore (even by a Hong Kong company) are not taxed in Hong Kong. Less welcoming countries try to cast the net wider. Several US states have flirted with unitary taxation, which allows the tax authorities to bring a taxpayer's worldwide profits within the tax net. So if you set up a subsidiary company in California, the taxman there might seek to tax your group's worldwide profits, not just the profits of your Californian subsidiary. Fortunately, even the pioneering legislators of California have realised that unitary taxation is a disincentive to inward investment and have softened their stance, but this type of issue should be watched carefully as tax regimes change rapidly with annual finance and tax statutes. Other jurisdictions have a different focus. Russia and several East European countries impose hefty tax burdens on the hiring of staff, with social security payments amounting to a large percentage of an employee's salary. Others use sales tax to raise revenue. Whichever country you choose, you must check the tax position before deciding on your legal and operational structure.

Employment. Many US and Far Eastern businesses coming to Europe are not prepared for the extensive employment-protection laws commonly found there. The US system allows employers wide scope in hiring and firing staff, subject to some basic restraints on wrongful dismissal and more extensive controls on racial and sexual discrimination. European employees typically have entrenched rights which allow them substantial compensation if the employer seeks to end their employment for purely economic reasons.

Agency arrangements. An attractive option for extending a sales effort into new territories is to use a network of agents to represent your business, market your products and act on your behalf. This avoids the expense and commitment of establishing your own presence in the territory, and allows you to plug into an established trading operation with someone who should know the local scene. But you should check out any laws that protect the rights of agents; in the European Union agents are guaranteed a measure of compensation if the principal ends the relationship.

Product liability. You will be familiar with the management of the risk attaching to your goods or services in your home market, but you should not assume the rules are the same everywhere. Once again, the European Union has rules that extend potential liability beyond what is commonly understood in the USA. Other jurisdictions have their own, idiosyncratic regulations which require close scrutiny.

Exchange controls. Some emerging economies have restrictions on the free transfer of capital in and out of the country. Others are happy to let it in, but place limits on taking it out. It would be embarrassing to struggle to get a foreign business off the ground, only to find that you cannot repatriate your profits or can do so only on payment of unexpected taxes.

Exchange risk. Currency fluctuations plague international traders. The best projections can be shattered by uncontrollable changes in exchange rates. The risks become more acute if you establish a foreign currency cost-base that you have to support from home.

Political risk. This covers a wide range of issues, but anyone considering a cross-border venture should think about the political and economic stability of the chosen territory. Many political changes are unforeseeable, but others are more predictable and prudent entrepreneurs will take soundings on the business climate.

These points should not put you off; they should just make you a little wary. Cross-border trade and overseas investment are vital components of diversification and expansion, but you need to know the risks – both legal and economic – before you embark on a foreign venture.

How to Pick a Good Lawyer

It is a personal thing, of course, but there must be a difference between a good and a bad lawyer. Some lawyers consistently have more success than others, in the sense that they win more cases or pull off more deals – and make more money. Some lawyers are undoubtedly cleverer than their rivals, but does brain power alone make a good lawyer? Personal flair and an ability to attract clients are probably more valuable attributes. Most lawyers seem to work hard and are dedicated to their profession, so mere hard work and dedication does not make the difference between a blooming flower and a shrivelling weed. What marks out one lawyer above another? How can you shift through the bunch to pick the best? And is the acknowledged best really the best for you?

Here are a few ideas to think about.

A good stable. It is not a litmus test, but the better lawyers tend to seek out each other and join together in successful firms. An exceptional lawyer will not stay long in a mediocre firm and a mediocre lawyer will not last long in an exceptional firm. Partnerships are strange and have many shortcomings, but one strength is the personal involvement and commitment of every partner. If a member of the firm is not up to the same standard as the rest, he or she will have to go. If not, the reputation of the whole firm will suffer. Although you cannot assume that all the lawyers in a firm are as good as each other, you can take a measure of comfort from a law firm's good reputation and the necessity to protect and nurture that reputation.

Horses for courses. Lawyers who claim to practice in a wide field are inevitably generalists. As such, they will not have the same level of expertise in all the areas they cover and will not have the same depth of knowledge as true specialists. Some legal jobs are well suited to a generalist, but more complex issues require special skills and you would be wise to find a specialist lawyer to tackle them. Legal directories are useful guides and spell out the leaders in their recognised fields. Beyond that, you have to ask around to find the best bet.

Availability. You need a lawyer who makes himself available to you. It is no good if he is never around to take your calls or invariably sends a stand-in to meetings because he is too busy with other work. In deciding whether he will give you the necessary level of service, you need to take a realistic view of his priorities. If your corporate lawyer is about to embark on the flotation of a massive enterprise, you are fooling yourself if you think he is going to give you priority for your franchise agreement. With busy commercial lawyers, you need to make a judgement about their assistants and support staff, since inevitably you will be relying on them to a large extent.

Personal style. If your company has a public image as a caring, customer-oriented, considerate organisation, you probably do not want to hire a rottweiler as a lawyer for your contract negotiations (although you might for your debt-collection work). However, as a corporate raider, you might like the idea of the nastiest attorney in town. It is a matter of personal taste, but at least you should find out what sort of personality you are hiring before you decide it is the right one for you.

Ability to communicate. There is a general feeling that the better lawyers are better communicators. A brilliant legal mind is wasted if it is housed in a withdrawn, reclusive personality that cannot put across a message in a convincing and effective manner. Success in the law depends on an ability to get on with people, to work well in a team and to convince people to do things they might otherwise prefer not to do. Negotiation of a commercial deal or pursuit of a litigation case requires communication skills, so choose a lawyer who passes the test.

Confidence. If your lawyer does not inspire confidence in you at your first meeting, he is likely to make the same impression (or lack of it) on other people. Remember that this person will be carrying your banner; the other side will make a judgement on you from the actions and appearance of your lawyer. If your lawyer lacks confidence, they might assume that there is an acknowledged flaw in your case or a lack of conviction in your will to win. If your lawyer exudes confidence, you have scored a big point with the other side. It makes you feel better, too.

Reputation. You will not be the first potential client to wonder if this lawyer is the one for you. Check him out. Ask around. If you do not know anyone who has used him before, ask the lawyer himself if you can talk to any of his established clients. He will almost certainly agree. Ask about his bad points as well as the good ones. Press and probe. Work out what factors are important to you and build some questions around them. Take up a full reference.

When looking for a lawyer, knowledge of the law is assumed. Most people want a purposeful, practical character who will not waste their money with pyrrhic victories or ill-thought-out strategies. They want personal service, good communication and a personal style that suits their own. Some people do not want a lawyer who drives a Ferrari; others do. Some do not like law firms with excessive marble (or fountains) in the reception area; others do. Some do not like chalk-stripe suits with ill-matching ties and braces (suspenders); others think they are prerequisite for a good corporate lawyer. Whatever your preferences, there is no substitute for trying out someone and working with them to see if you operate well as a team, preferably a winning one.

Part 2

A–Z

A FORTIORI

A Latin expression used by pompous lawyers to mean "for a compelling reason", as in: if he is a pompous lawyer, then *a fortiori* he uses expressions like this.

ABA

See AMERICAN BAR ASSOCIATION.

ACCEPTANCE

One of the conditions that must be satisfied to form a valid CONTRACT, acceptance is the act of notifying the other party that you agree to the terms of his OFFER, thereby creating the contract.

ACCORD AND SATISFACTION

When a debtor pays off a debt, and the creditor accepts the payment in full and final settlement, the payment is said to be in accord and satisfaction of the debt. This bars the creditor from suing the debtor. (See also RELEASE AND DISCHARGE.)

ACCUSATORIAL PROCEDURE

This is the criminal judicial system adopted by countries such as the UK and the USA, whereby the prosecution gathers the evidence against the accused and presents it to the court as the supposed facts of how the accused committed the crime. The accused then has to produce contrary evidence to defend himself or may simply hope that the prosecution has not done enough to convince the JURY (or the JUDGE, if there is no jury) that the supposed facts were the true facts. In contrast, the CIVIL CODE relies on the INQUISITORIAL PROCEDURE whereby a MAGISTRATE is given the task of investigating the case and producing the evidence to the court.

ACKNOWLEDGEMENT OF SERVICE

A document confirming SERVICE OF PROCESS of a WRIT or SUMMONS, in other words that it has been received by the DEFENDANT, and intimating that the defendant intends to defend the action.

ACT OF PARLIAMENT
A STATUTE passed into law by PARLIAMENT.

People must not do things for fun. We are not here for fun. There is no reference to fun in any Act of Parliament.
A.P. Herbert, 1935

ACTUAL NOTICE
To have NOTICE of something, meaning to be aware of it, by virtue of your own knowledge either because you have seen it yourself or you have been told by someone. Actual notice may be a good defence to an action for MISREPRESENTATION, since if you knew the true facts you cannot claim to have been misled by the misrepresented facts. (See also CONSTRUCTIVE NOTICE.)

ADMINISTRATION (LETTERS OF)
When someone dies and leaves a valid WILL, a person appointed under the will to administer the deceased person's estate is an EXECUTOR. The appointment of executors is confirmed and given legal blessing by a document (the grant of PROBATE) issued by the court. However, if there is no will to be found or the executors named in the will cannot or refuse to act, the court will issue another document (always referred to in the plural as letters of administration) to empower someone (the administrator) to deal with the deceased's estate as if he were an executor.

Nobody has a more sacred obligation to obey the law than those who make the law.
Jean Anouilh, 1942

ADMINISTRATIVE LAW
Known in North America and elsewhere as regulatory law, in the UK administrative law covers the rules that control how governments and governmental agencies govern the people. There is a long list of cases where citizens have successfully

challenged the might of the executive in the courts (see JUDICIAL REVIEW).

AD VALOREM

This Latin phrase, meaning literally "to the value of", is used to signify one value in proportion to another. For example, *ad valorem* STAMP DUTY is charged at 0.5% of the value of shares transferred in a UK company. The amount of tax payable is proportional to the value of the shares transferred.

ADVERSE POSSESSION

Squatter's rights, where someone is in possession of land contrary to the rights of the true owner. If you maintain adverse possession for long enough (say, 12 years) without complaint from the owner, you can acquire legal ownership. This is known as POSSESSORY TITLE.

AFFIDAVIT

From the Latin "he has said it". The law often turns to Latin for a weighty phrase to enhance the substance of something quite straightforward. An affidavit is a written statement of evidence used in court proceedings. To remind the person of the seriousness of court evidence, an affidavit is given a Latin name and has to be sworn in the presence of a SOLICITOR or COMMISSIONER FOR OATHS by holding a bible and uttering the words: "I swear by Almighty God that this is my name and handwriting and that the contents of this, my affidavit, are true." (See also AFFIRMATION and OATH.)

AFFIRMATION

A solemn declaration that what you are about to say is true, but without swearing an OATH.

AGENCY

An agreement whereby one party agrees to act on behalf of another (the PRINCIPAL) for an agreed purpose. A sales agent acts on behalf of its principal in selling goods or services to customers. A collecting agent receives money from customers on behalf of its principal. The important part of the agency relationship is the extent of authority granted by the principal to the agent. Full authority means that the agent has the power to enter into a CONTRACT on behalf of the principal and to bind it contractually without its further involvement. In contrast, a principal may authorise its agent to procure orders only for contracts, so the principal reserves the right to accept or decline the orders and thus decides for itself whether to accept a binding contract. Where an agent sells goods on behalf of a principal, such as a REAL ESTATE agent (realtor), the agent never acquires TITLE to the goods or property. When a contract for the sale of something is concluded, title passes from the principal to the buyer. This distinguishes an agency from a DISTRIBUTORSHIP. A distributor buys the goods from the supplier, acquires title to them, and resells them on its own account, thereby acting as a principal itself (see EXCLUSIVE).

ALLOTMENT LETTER
See LETTER OF ALLOTMENT.

ALTERNATE DIRECTOR
A DIRECTOR who is unable to fulfil his role, perhaps because of absence from the country, may appoint someone to stand in his place. Alternate directors exercise the same powers as the person who appoints them and the appointment can be short or long term. An alternate director must be registered at COMPANIES HOUSE in the same way as a director.

ALTERNATIVE DISPUTE RESOLUTION
Or ADR – see MEDIATION.

AMERICAN BAR ASSOCIATION
If anyone can throw a good party, the American Bar Association (ABA) can. This organisation of lawyers from across the USA meets every year at a different location to discuss hot topics of legal practice. The most ardent of the ABA's party-goers graduate to the global league of the INTERNATIONAL BAR ASSOCIATION.

A

ANCIENT LIGHTS

An EASEMENT or right to claim an entitlement to adequate light to the windows of your property. Thus as an owner of REAL ESTATE you can object to your neighbour erecting a building that denies adequate light to your building.

Lawyers... persons who write a 10,000 word document and call it a brief.
Louis Brandeis

ANTI-TRUST

Originally a US term used to describe the campaign to dismantle monopolistic trusts or trading cartels that artificially protected the prices of commodities, such as oil, against the competitive forces of free trade, it has come to be used around the world to describe any legislation or action against monopolies or anti-competitive practices. The most potent anti-trust force in Europe is the legislation incorporated in Articles 85 and 86 of the TREATY OF ROME, which founded what has developed into the European Union (EU). This legislation gives powers to the European Commission and the courts of member states to take action against non-competitive practices affecting EU trade.

ANTON PILLAR

Taken from the name of a UK case, this is a court order granted only in exceptional (but increasingly frequent) circumstances to allow a PLAINTIFF powers of search and seizure of documents against the DEFENDANT. It is exceptional because the application for an Anton Pillar order is heard by a JUDGE EX PARTE, that is without the defendant being represented or being given a chance to state its side of the story. This is justified on the ground that if it knew about the proceedings, the defendant would be likely to destroy the evidence on which the plaintiff relies to establish its case. Before granting such powers and to ensure the balance of fairness, the judge needs to be convinced that the circumstances are appropriate and will impose strict restrictions on the plaintiff. These include a time limit for bringing both parties before the court, some security for the defendant's costs if the plaintiff fails to justify its action at the substantive (main) hearing, a precise definition of the evidence to be seized (to prevent a fishing expedition by the plaintiff) and the appointment of an independent lawyer to supervise the raid. Nevertheless, the powers of an Anton Pillar order are striking and present a valuable weapon for the serious-minded litigant. They also provide a marvellous opportunity for swashbuckling LITIGATION lawyers to lead their assault troops in a dawn attack, with much splintering of door frames and whoops of excitement, at somebody else's expense.

> *Lawyers are like rhinoceroses: thick-skinned,*
> *short-sighted and always ready to charge.*
> David Mellor, MP

APPEAL

To ask a higher or more senior court to review and, if it thinks fit, reverse a decision of a lower court. In the UK appeals from the court of FIRST INSTANCE go to the Court of Appeal and thereafter, with the leave of the court, to the Judicial Committee of the House of Lords (the upper house of the UK PARLIAMENT). Leave to appeal to the House of Lords is given only for an issue that has special importance or has wider implications beyond those of the particular case. The USA has a similar system of appeals, within the federal and state jurisdictions, with the SUPREME COURT as the final court of appeal.

ARBITRATION

This is a form of dispute resolution that does not use the court system, but otherwise (and increasingly) follows generally accepted LITIGATION procedures. It is more formal than MEDIATION but has some common characteristics. All parties to the dispute must agree to have the issue resolved by this method; no one can be forced to take part without agreement. All parties must agree to the selection of an arbitrator, who will decide between the competing claims. The arbitrator is usually an expert in the field of the dispute, although most arbitration agreements contain a provision for a specified third party to nominate the arbitrator if the parties cannot agree. All parties must agree to the location of the hearing, the language of the proceedings and the procedural rules to be used. Around the world various trade bodies have encapsulated arbitration rules in published codes, which the parties can adopt by simple reference in their arbitration agreement. The International Chamber of Commerce (ICC) rules are perhaps the most well known. Popular venues are those with easy access for the parties and, especially in international disputes, countries with noted neutrality. A good selection of fancy restaurants and tempting night-life may also influence the choice because of their attractions to the hordes of lawyers who will descend on the proceedings.

Arbitration is often mistakenly assumed to be a cheaper alternative to courtroom litigation. This may have been true in the past, when a dispute in a specialist area of business was readily referred to an accepted father of the industry for a speedy decision, which the parties were happy to accept. In recent years, however, lawyers have hijacked the arbitration process and brought it firmly back into the realms of litigation. Not surprisingly, the time scale turns out to be the same: one party's lawyer does not want to fall down on the thoroughness of his client's case by taking a short cut or ignoring an issue merely because the proceedings are supposedly less formal than a courtroom trial. Equally unsurprisingly, the costs turn out to be the same: except that you have to pay for an arbitrator, whereas you get a JUDGE for free.

On balance, there are probably only three good reasons to prefer arbitration to the courtroom:

- where the dispute is so technical, or the industry is so idiosyncratic, that the parties do not trust a common-or-garden judge to understand the vital issues;

- for confidentiality since, unlike in the courts, the parties can agree to wash their dirty linen in the privacy of the arbitration room;
- in international disputes, to avoid forcing one party to submit to the courts of the other's home jurisdiction. As every footballer knows, playing away from home in front of a hostile crowd can be a distinct disadvantage.

ARTICLES OF ASSOCIATION

These are the bylaws of a UK company, which govern its internal constitution, in contrast to its MEMORANDUM OF ASSOCIATION, which governs its powers for dealing with outsiders. The articles cover issues such as the rights attaching to the company's shares, procedures for the transfer of shares, arrangements for general meetings, the appointment and removal of directors, procedures for board meetings and so on. Many private companies adopt a standard form of articles set out in the COMPANIES ACTS, known universally as TABLE A. A resolution to change a company's articles must be a SPECIAL RESOLUTION.

ASSIGNMENT

The assignment of a right is its transfer from one person to another. To be fully effective – an absolute assignment – it must be in writing signed by both parties, without any qualification or reservation over the right transferred and with appropriate notice to any party against whom the right can be enforced. Thus if A owes £10 to B, B can assign its debt to C by entering into an assignment with C and giving appropriate notice to A. (Contrast an assignment with a LICENCE and a NOVATION.)

ATTACHMENT OF EARNINGS

An order of a court to take money on a regular basis from a person's salary to satisfy a court fine or a judgement debt owed to another person. (See also GARNISHEE ORDER.)

ATTESTATION
The attestation clause in a CONTRACT or DEED is the part showing that the signatures of the parties have been witnessed. It usually says something along the lines of "signed by John Smith in the presence of…". The witness will then sign, add his or her name and address, and sometimes his or her profession.

ATTORNEY
Someone who is authorised to act on behalf of somebody else (as in POWER OF ATTORNEY). The title has also become commonly known as the abbreviation of attorney-at-law, meaning a lawyer acting on behalf of a client or simply a practising lawyer.

There are two kinds of lawyers, those who know the law and those who know the judge.
Charles Lamb

ATTORNEY-GENERAL
In the UK the attorney-general is one of the LAW OFFICERS of the Crown. He or she (but so far it has always been a he) will be a member of PARLIAMENT and is appointed to the position by the government of the day. The attorney-general advises the government on legal matters and has a say in deciding whether major prosecutions should be brought. In the USA the attorney-general is the head of legal affairs in a state or federal government. The attorney-general in the US federal government is head of the Department of Justice and is appointed by the president.

AUTHORISED CAPITAL
See NOMINAL CAPITAL.

BAILMENT

Not to be confused with bail, which comes from an altogether different department of the law, bailment is a wondrous concept devised (in the days when lawyers had nothing better to do than devise wondrous concepts) to describe an everyday situation. It is a good example of the law's need to cover every aspect of life. Bailment explains the legal relationship created when you part with your property temporarily but always intend to get it back. A good example is taking your suit to the dry cleaners. You are happy to hand it over to the cleaner, but there is an implied understanding that it will be handed back, preferably cleaned, later. The relationship of parting with possession of an item (a chattel), but not parting with ownership, is bailment. The owner is known as the bailor, the recipient the bailee, and the document (if there is one) that records the terms of the bailment (in our example the dry cleaner's receipt ticket) is called the bailment note. The parties can, of course, agree whatever terms they wish for the bailment note but only rarely do you see a customer at the dry cleaners conducting negotiations for the bailment terms other than price.

In other areas of business bailment plays a more valued role. In the jewellery trade, for example, precious stones are sent to be cut on the strength of a bailment note. If something goes amiss the value of the stone means it is probably worth going to a lawyer to learn more about the law of bailment.

BANKRUPTCY

A declaration by a court that a person is not able to pay his debts and, to protect him from further attacks by his creditors, that his affairs should be administered by another person (called the TRUSTEE IN BANKRUPTCY). In the UK the term bankruptcy should strictly be applied to individuals with the word INSOLVENCY used for companies, but common use (and general use in the USA) makes it applicable to both. The role of the trustee is to gather in the bankrupt's assets, convert them into cash and pay off the creditors as far as possible. Invariably the creditors get less than they are owed. At the end of this process, which may take several years as the bankrupt pays off some of his debt, the court will release (discharge) the bankrupt and allow him to start afresh with a clean sheet, all claims by the declared creditors being wiped away. Until he is discharged, a bankrupt in the UK cannot sign a contract on his own behalf, borrow money, act as a DIRECTOR of a company or serve as a member of PARLIAMENT.

In the USA a bankrupt corporation can apply to the court for protection from its creditors under Chapter 11 of the Bankruptcy Code and claim a breathing space to reorganise its affairs (for example, restructure its finances) while continuing to trade. If it is successful in sorting out its problems, it can emerge from Chapter 11 and resume normal life. If not, it will be forced into LIQUIDATION. This process can take some time; during the 1980s several US airlines continued to trade in Chapter 11 for years.

Law is to the litigant what the poulterer is to the goose; it plucks and draws him. But here the simile ends. For the litigant, unlike the goose, never gets any trust, although he may be roasted and dished.
John Willock, 1887

BARE TRUST
See TRUST.

BAR
The collective term for barristers or, in the USA, all lawyers.

BAR EXAMINATION
To practise as a BARRISTER in the UK you have to pass the qualifying examinations set by the INNS OF COURT. To practise as a lawyer in the USA you must satisfy the local requirements of a particular state, where the qualification process culminates

in a series of examinations set by the state BAR authorities. Some of these bar exams are notoriously difficult, with a high failure rate. Some states offer reciprocal or fast-track qualification for lawyers who have passed the bar exam of another state, but they all like to keep firm control over the qualification of their lawyers.

BARRISTER

The duality of the legal profession in the UK, as the distinction between barristers and solicitors is called, is confusing for British people, let alone foreigners. Whenever you point to a distinguishing feature, there is a ready example to contradict it. Everyone knows that the barrister is the one in the wig who stands up in court, but some never go to court at all or only rarely. Some think that the barrister is the cleverer lawyer (as solicitors take their clients to see the barrister for a definitive view on a particular topic of law), but there are one or two clever solicitors too. Many think that barristers earn a fortune, but a lot of them are struggling to make it pay. As with many UK institutions, it is a conundrum.

Taking an analogy from the medical profession, solicitors are the general practitioners. Typically, a SOLICITOR works in a firm with other solicitors (often in PARTNERSHIP) offering general legal services to clients: REAL ESTATE transactions, settling disputes, commercial business, family issues, inheritance work, tax planning and so on. Following the medical analogy, the barrister would be the consultant with expertise in a specific field, offering his or her services as an independent contractor (although usually operating from a communal office, known as a SET OF CHAMBERS, with other barristers). To get an expert view on a narrow topic of law, the solicitor may consult a barrister, frequently with the client, at a formal meeting known as a conference (or, if the barrister is a QUEEN'S COUNSEL, a consultation).

Many solicitors have little to do with barristers, but LITIGATION solicitors work closely with them in preparing a client's case for ultimate presentation to a court. Solicitors have always had the right to appear and speak in lower courts, but recently this right of audience has been extended to the higher courts. This prompts speculation that the duality may be nearing its end, as some fear that barristers will be swallowed up by solicitors. On the other hand, entrenched positions established over centuries tend not to disappear overnight.

He is no lawyer who cannot take two sides.
Anon

BEARER INSTRUMENT
A bundle of rights encapsulated in a document that can be transferred by simply passing it from one person to another; for example, a bank note.

BENEFICIAL INTEREST
The interest of a BENEFICIARY in property held under a TRUST.

BENEFICIARY
Someone who benefits under a TRUST or a WILL.

BEQUEST
A gift of property, but not land (which is a DEVISE), to someone under a WILL.

BILL
Before LEGISLATION emerges as an ACT OF PARLIAMENT or a STATUTE, it passes through PARLIAMENT (in the UK) or CONGRESS (in the USA) as a bill. The bill is debated in Parliament or Congress, amended in the course of the debates and ultimately voted on. In the UK a bill must receive the ROYAL ASSENT before passing into law; in the USA it must get the signature of the president.

BIMBO
A decorous acronym for buy-in/management buy-out. This is supposed to mean a combination of a MANAGEMENT BUY-IN and a MANAGEMENT BUY-OUT, which means an acquisition of a company by a

team comprising its existing management and outside managers.

BLUE BAG

A quintessentially British legal knick-knack, this is blue cloth bag with a string-pull in which a junior BARRISTER carries his wig and gown. Rather like a schoolboy's games kit bag, some blue bags bear the embroidered initials of the owner. As an important mark of career advancement, a junior barrister may be awarded a red bag by a QUEEN'S COUNSEL in return for effort and endeavour in a particular case. This is a badge of distinction and may be carried with a swagger. It is like being awarded school colours.

BLUE PENCIL

The mythical blue pencil is wielded by a JUDGE, or anyone else, trying to make sense of a provision in a CONTRACT, which is either nonsense or part of which is contrary to a principle of law. If the provision can be given an effective legal meaning by deleting some words, the blue pencil will be used to delete them. This enables judges (or other individuals) to ignore the words they consider otiose and give effect to the remainder.

BONA VACANTIA

Vacant goods? Property with no evident owner, such as TREASURE TROVE or the ESTATE of someone who dies without leaving any heirs, which usually passes to the state.

Mrs Bertram: *That sounds like nonsense, my dear.*
Mr Bertram: *May be so, my dear, but it may be
very good law for all that.*
Sir Walter Scott

BOND

A ubiquitous term, hijacked long ago by the marketing arm of the financial services industry, used to enhance the substance of insubstantial obligations. A bond is really nothing more than a

---

promise or obligation to do something, usually to pay money.

- A government bond is a promise by a sovereign state to pay an amount of money on a particular date. Its substance derives from that of the government, not of the security itself.
- A bearer bond is an obligation to pay the holder of the bond and does not have any name written on it.
- A MORTGAGE bond is a certificate that a mortgage exists on certain property.
- Goods held in bond are held by customs authorities until excise duties or other taxes are paid on them.

The large number of securities and investment products with the word bond in their names are nothing more than a bare promise to pay money.

BONDED WAREHOUSE
A storage facility for imported goods to be held in bond (that is, under the control of the customs authorities) until the appropriate customs duties have been paid.

BONUS ISSUE
A step beyond a RIGHTS ISSUE, where a company offers its shareholders the right to buy new shares in proportion to the number of shares they currently hold. A bonus issue gives away the new shares (fully paid up) without requiring any payment, by capitalising (converting into SHARE capital) accumulated reserves (profits) of the company.

BRIEF
The bundle of papers, traditionally bound up in pink ribbon, delivered by a SOLICITOR to a BARRISTER setting out a client's case and giving instructions for the barrister to follow at trial or in preparation for a trial. By some strange linguistic extension, it has become a slang term for any sort of lawyer (particularly a barrister).

BURDEN OF PROOF

This is the duty of parties in LITIGATION to prove their case, in other words to prove that their evidence is true or that the other side's evidence is false. The standard of proof – the extent to which a party has to prove its case – is different for criminal and civil cases. To secure a conviction in a criminal case, the prosecution must show that the defendant is guilty "beyond all reasonable doubt". This is a heavier burden than in a civil case, where the PLAINTIFF must prove his or her case "on the balance of probabilities".

> *A just cause needs no interpreting. It carries its own case. But the unjust argument, since it is sick, needs clever medicine.*
> Euripides, 411 BC

BUSINESS ANGEL

An expression borrowed from the theatrical world meaning a private investor in a small company. As well as providing EQUITY CAPITAL or DEBT FINANCE, the business angel often contributes his personal expertise to the business as a NON-EXECUTIVE DIRECTOR.

C

Call option

A contractual right to require someone to sell something to you. Details of the length of time the right remains open (the option period) and a mechanism to determine the purchase price (the option price) will be set out in a CONTRACT. The reverse of a call option, that is the right to require someone to buy something from you, is a PUT OPTION.

Caps and collars

These expressions refer to clauses in financing documents that limit the extent to which interest charges on borrowed funds can rise (cap) or fall (collar) notwithstanding fluctuations in base rates.

Case law

A fundamental principle of COMMON LAW, case law is law established by precedent, which means the decisions of courts in earlier cases. Precedents apply unless and until they are overruled by a higher court or overtaken by LEGISLATION enacted by PARLIAMENT.

All bad precedents began as justifiable measures.
Julius Caesar, 100 BC

Caveat emptor

Meaning "buyer beware", this is another helpful Latin expression that is used where an English one would do nicely. It means that the seller is giving NO WARRANTY or other contractual comfort over the goods or property it is about to sell. The buyer must make its own investigations and must take the ensuing RISK of any flaw or defect. It is a tough world out there.

Chancery Division

A division of the HIGH COURT, the Chancery Division deals with wills, inheritance claims, companies, taxation, LIQUIDATION, BANKRUPTCY and other issues that can be extremely dry and tedious, but that demand the painstaking attention of some of the cleverest lawyers. Romantics may think of Charles Dickens and *Bleak House*.

CHARGE

A form of SECURITY given in support of a debt. Where a borrower gives a lender a charge over an asset, the lender has the right to seize the asset if the borrower fails to repay the debt on the agreed terms. A legal charge (or legal MORTGAGE) is where the relationship is formalised and the chargee's or mortgagee's interest is recorded against the asset, for example, in the TITLE deeds to REAL ESTATE. An equitable charge is more informal, such as the deposit of title deeds with the chargee to prevent the disposal of the asset rather than full registration of the chargee's interest. This is another example of where EQUITY will recognise a legal relationship which falls below the precise requirements set by COMMON LAW. Every charge given by a UK company must be registered at COMPANIES HOUSE within 15 days of its creation, otherwise it may not be enforceable against a liquidator if the company were subsequently to enter into LIQUIDATION.

CHARGE CERTIFICATE

See LAND CERTIFICATE.

CIF

The acronym for cost, insurance, freight. Similar to FOB, this is an expression used in international trade contracts for the supply of goods. It means that the seller is responsible for arranging the insurance, carriage and delivery of the goods to the agreed destination.

CIVIL CODE

See below.

CIVIL LAW

The foundation of the legal system used in continental Europe. Codified on the instructions of Napoleon, and often referred to as the civil code, it draws much from ROMAN LAW as well as European jurisprudential thinking. It is quite distinct from the anglocentric system of COMMON LAW. Unlike common law, it avoids the theory of precedent (where the decision of one court will be applied in another court unless and until it is overruled by a higher court) and dislikes laws that are not written down (codified). Shared labels (like the term GOOD FAITH) can have significantly different meanings.

CLOSING
The US equivalent of COMPLETION.

COLLATERAL
A US term used to mean SECURITY in the sense of some form of CHARGE or guarantee that a debtor will pay its debt. It derives from a collateral contract, that is, a contract sitting side-by-side with another contract and relating to it. Thus a borrower (the debtor) will enter into a loan agreement, which details the terms of the loan, and also a collateral agreement, such as a MORTGAGE or a GUARANTEE, to provide security for the repayment of the loan.

COMFORT LETTER
A letter or other document passing between two parties, often related to a CONTRACT, whereby one party gives an assurance to the other that it will do or not do something. The vital point is that the assurance is not meant to be legally binding. It is something like a GENTLEMEN'S AGREEMENT. I promise not to do such and such, but you cannot sue me if I do. So in truth it is not much comfort.

COMMISSIONER FOR OATHS
Someone officially appointed to administer an OATH relating to a formal document, such as an AFFIDAVIT of evidence to be presented to a court. In the UK a SOLICITOR can act as a commissioner for oaths, but, to maintain a position of independence, he or she should not take an oath for his or her own client.

C

COMMITTAL PROCEEDINGS

A preliminary step in the court process for a major criminal prosecution, committal proceedings take place at a hearing before a MAGISTRATE who decides whether the case is sufficiently serious (and whether the prosecution has established a PRIMA FACIE case) for it to be transferred to a higher court for a full trial.

The law, in its majestic equality, forbids the rich, as well as the poor, to sleep under the bridges, to beg in the streets, and to steal bread.

Anatole France

COMMON LAW

A system of law, used in England, Commonwealth countries and the USA based on the principle of applying precedent set by previous judicial decisions. Common law is distinct from CIVIL LAW. Courts will interpret the legal analysis in a case by reference to decisions of earlier cases involving analogous circumstances. Judges are bound to follow the rationale of earlier decisions unless they see sufficient reasons to distinguish the current facts from the previous facts. The only departure from this principle is that a higher court may overrule a decision of a lower court, thereby creating a new precedent in place of the previous one. Common law is supplemented (and also overridden) by STATUTE law, laid down by LEGISLATION.

Although the doctrine of following precedent is admired to the extent that it provides certainty for others to follow, it restricts judges from taking into account the changing nature of society and can lead to injustice. In the UK the most celebrated opponent of slavish devotion to precedent has been Lord Denning, who until his retirement in the late 1980s was the most prominent JUDGE of his era. Throughout his legal career he made an art of avoiding the strictures of precedent where he felt it tended towards injustice. Strongly opposed by common law purists at the time and since, his legacy is a number of legal principles (often based on the principles of EQUITY) which were created out of arguments to avoid the tight corner of precedent. These principles are now, of course, enshrined in precedent.

COMMUNITY PROPERTY

In contrast to SEPARATE PROPERTY, which a husband and wife acquire before their marriage and continue to own separately, community property is property acquired during the course of a marriage and deemed to be owned jointly by them. The odd thing about this concept is that while it is firmly established in the COMMON LAW jurisdiction of the USA and the CIVIL LAW jurisdiction of continental Europe and many other countries around the world, it is not recognised in English law. The UK divorce courts have to rely on the principles of EQUITY (with some help from STATUTE) to override the strict rules of ownership laid down by common law in order to reach a fair division of a married couple's assets.

> *It usually takes a hundred years to make a law, and then, after it has done its work, it usually takes a hundred years to get rid of it.*
> Henry Ward Beecher, 1887

COMPANIES ACTS

The statutes that govern the basic affairs of all UK companies. Commencing in the 18th century, they have been changed and supplemented throughout history. The latest consolidation is the Companies Act 1985, but the continuous temptation for governments to tinker with this chapter of LEGISLATION means it is constantly on the move.

COMPANIES HOUSE

A quaint term used to describe the governmental agency that provides the regulatory framework for UK companies. Every company incorporated in the UK must be registered. Every company must register its corporate details, such as the identity of its directors and MEMBERS. Every CHARGE or MORTGAGE

C

on a company's property must be registered. All these registrations are made at Companies House.

COMPANY LIMITED BY GUARANTEE

A limited liability company that does not have shares. The liability of the MEMBERS is limited to the amount that they have agreed to guarantee to the company. This type of company is frequently used for charitable organisations, where the members do not expect (and often are prohibited from receiving) any return from their investment in the company.

COMPANY LIMITED BY SHARES

A limited liability company that issues shares to its MEMBERS. The liability of the members is limited to the amount, if any, unpaid on the shares held.

COMPANY SEARCH

The act of viewing the public record of information on a company. In the UK such records are maintained by the REGISTRAR OF COMPANIES at COMPANIES HOUSE. A company search is usually carried out by commercial search agencies. The available information includes the identity of the company's MEMBERS and directors, its corporate structure, any registered charges or mortgages and its annual accounts.

COMPETITION LAW

See ANTI-TRUST and the TREATY OF ROME.

COMPLETION

When the parties sign and exchange a CONTRACT, they fix their respective obligations and become bound to carry them out. Some contracts, such as for the sale and purchase of REAL ESTATE, anticipate certain events taking place after exchange but before the intent behind the contract is fulfilled; for example, before the TITLE to the real estate passes. When post-contractual conditions are fulfilled, the contract is completed (and title passes); hence completion of the contract. In US legal jargon, the contract is said to be closed and the equivalent to completion is CLOSING.

CONGRESS

The legislative body of many countries, notably the USA, where it is made up of the House of Representatives (lower house) and the Senate (upper house). With its written constitution and strong dedication to the SEPARATION OF POWERS, the US system looks far removed from the UK PARLIAMENT on which it was based.

CONSIDERATION

This is one of the necessary components of a CONTRACT. The party seeking to enforce an agreement as a legally binding contract must show that it did something, or expressly did not do something, in return for the other party's promise to do something or not do something. This element of something in return is called consideration. It can be nominal (such as a PEPPERCORN), but it must be there in some form and the party relying on the contract must show that it was provided; hence another unforgettable legal maxim that "consideration must move from the promisee". There is one qualification. If the agreement is written under SEAL (that is, it is a DEED not merely a contract), there is no need for consideration. The law interprets this extra degree of formality as sufficient evidence that the parties intended their agreement to be legally binding.

> *Good laws, if they are not obeyed, do not constitute good government.*
> Aristotle, 400 BC

CONSPIRACY

This is a crime, established at COMMON LAW over the centuries, with bumpy edges. In simple terms, a conspiracy is an agreement between two or more people to commit a crime. Difficulties arise over the seriousness of the conspiracy: it is one thing to conspire to commit murder, another to conspire to park illegally in a no-waiting zone. Both are conspiracies and, technically, are dealt with by the same rules. Liberal jurists worry that prosecuting authorities use a charge of conspiracy when there is insufficient evidence to secure a conviction on the substantive crime; in our examples, murder and illegal parking. It is an allegation of evil thoughts, not necessarily evil deeds. You can be convicted of conspiracy to murder without killing, or even harming, anybody. This is dangerous ground.

CONSTRUCTIVE NOTICE

If you have ACTUAL NOTICE of something, you are aware of it by virtue of your own knowledge. However, in addition to your own knowledge, the law will assume in certain circumstances that you know about something (whether or not you actually do) because the information is readily available to you. In applying constructive notice, the law is imposing on you a duty to be prudent, for the benefit of others with whom you have dealings, so that you cannot complain if you suffer loss from failing to be prudent. For example, a large amount of information about UK companies is available on public record at COMPANIES HOUSE. A court will expect a prudent trader to inspect this information. If there is something on record that you ought to know, for example that the company has entered into LIQUIDATION, then this knowledge will be imputed to you by constructive notice and you cannot complain if you did not know or did not check.

CONTEMPT OF COURT

Showing disrespect to a court or disregard for a court order. If you are rude to a JUDGE in court or refuse to comply with the court's procedures, he can hold you "in contempt" and have you sent to prison until you "purge your contempt" (apologise). A breach of an INJUNCTION or any court order is a contempt of court.

CONTINGENCY FEE

Devised in the USA to make LITIGATION affordable to everyone, a contingency fee is charged by a lawyer to a client only if the lawyer is successful in winning the client's case and is calculated as a percentage of the DAMAGES recovered. It is commonly used in personal injury actions where the injured victim would not otherwise have the resources to hire a lawyer at normal commercial rates. With the contingency percentage at 30% or more, some lawyers have established lucrative businesses by seeking out accident victims and encouraging them to file a suit; hence the accusation of being ambulance chasers. This style of charging legal fees has been prohibited for UK lawyers for many years, but recently the rules have been relaxed. Solicitors and barristers may enter into conditional fee arrangements whereby they get increased fees if they win or no fees at all if they lose.

I have come to regard the law courts not as a cathedral but rather as a casino.

Richard Ingrams, when editor of the much-sued magazine *Private Eye*

CONTRACT

An agreement, written or oral, between two or more parties where one party undertakes to do something in return for something else. All systems of law have developed formulae to determine when a legal contract is formed. COMMON LAW focuses on an offer by one party, which is converted into a contract when accepted by another. In addition, the law requires that the parties should intend to be legally bound, thus distinguishing a contract from a GENTLEMEN'S AGREEMENT. The terms of the contract should be reasonably certain and the party seeking to rely on it must be able to show it has given CONSIDERATION. If all of these criteria are satisfied, you can enforce the contract. If one or more is not, you cannot.

Sam Goldwyn's famous remark that "an oral agreement is not worth the paper it is written on" is not true (even forgiving the nonsense), but it serves to remind us of the difficulties of proving the existence and terms of a contract if they are

---

not written down and signed by the parties. No doubt spurred on by Mr Goldwyn, the UK PARLIAMENT enacted LEGISLATION long ago which requires important contracts (in its view important means they involve shares or REAL ESTATE) to be written if they are to be valid.

Justice is incidental to law and order.
J. Edgar Hoover

CONTRIBUTORY NEGLIGENCE
Being held to have contributed to your own injury because of your own NEGLIGENCE. If you are a passenger in a car that is involved in an accident as a result of the negligence of the driver (or any other example of the TORT of negligence), you might sue the driver for DAMAGES for your injuries. However, if you had failed to wear your seat-belt and this had exacerbated the injuries you suffered, the driver might claim that you were guilty of contributory negligence in that you negligently contributed to your own injuries. If the court accepts this, it would assess the percentage by which your own negligence contributed to your injuries and reduce the level of damages awarded against the driver by this percentage.

CONVERTIBLE LOANS
These are loans to a company that on the occurrence of specified events (usually default) entitle the lender to convert the loan into EQUITY CAPITAL and thereby exercise some measure of control over the company through voting shares.

CONVEYANCE
The formal document that transfers the ownership of property, especially REAL ESTATE, from one person to another. Conveyancing is the law and procedure relating to the transfer of real estate. A conveyancer is a lawyer whose practice centres on real estate transactions. For something completely different, see the explanation of fraudulent conveyance under FRAUD.

COPYRIGHT

An INTELLECTUAL PROPERTY right, copyright is the concept of ownership in words or other things that can be written down or portrayed graphically. Copyright is created when it is first published, and publication means the merest intention to make the work public by recording it in a medium, such as on paper, for others to see. There is no copyright in an idea when it is just in your head, but you create copyright when you write it down and show it to someone. The primary owner of copyright is the person who first created it: the author, the composer, the artist.

The law has identified circumstances where the primary owner is treated as having created copyright for a secondary owner; for instance, copyright created by an employee in the course of employment is automatically vested in the employer. Copyright can be transferred by CONTRACT either before or after it is created. An outright transfer is an ASSIGNMENT. A limited transfer, where the owner retains some of the right by reference to geography or a time period or similar restriction, is a LICENCE. Income from a copyright assignment or licence is commonly called a ROYALTY.

Copyright law is struggling to cope with the emergence of new forms of media. This ancient concept relies on rules to determine when a work is physically published (that is, written down) and it does not easily adapt to the brave new world of computers where, to most eyes, the work never sees the light of day. There is much room for argument and much work for lawyers here.

Any society that needs disclaimers has too many lawyers.
Erik Pepke

CORONER

A public official in charge of an INQUEST into an untimely or unexpected death. A coroner is not a JUDGE in the usual sense, but acts in a judicial capacity in presiding over the proceedings and

---

directing the JURY on what it must decide. A coroner is often a SOLICITOR, a doctor or other professional who takes on this occasional role in addition to his or her professional duties. In the UK, as a somewhat bizarre departure from an inquest into a death, a coroner is also charged with the task of holding an inquest into a case of TREASURE TROVE.

COUNTY COURT
In the UK large civil claims are heard by the HIGH COURT. Smaller claims are heard by local courts known as County Courts.

CROSS EXAMINATION
In court, after witnesses have given their evidence in response to the EXAMINATION IN CHIEF presented by the lawyer for their side, they must answer questions put by the lawyer for the other side. This is cross examination.

CUM DIVIDEND
Where a SHARE is offered to a buyer cum dividend, it means the buyer will acquire it pregnant with dividend rights and the value of these rights is reflected in the price offered. In contrast, where a share is quoted EX DIVIDEND, the recently declared dividend will go to the seller and the price has been reduced accordingly.

CURE PERIOD
A period of time, specified in a CONTRACT, for one party to remedy a breach of its obligations when notified by the other party. Typically, it will be given a short period (say 30 days) to put things right before the other party is entitled to terminate the contract (see TERMINATION CLAUSE) and seek compensation for the breach.

DAMAGES

Monetary compensation claimed by (or awarded to) a PLAINTIFF from a DEFENDANT for a loss or injury caused by the defendant. The concept of damages as compensation for loss is at the heart of LITIGATION. If the plaintiff has not suffered any loss, even though the defendant has caused a wrong, the litigation will fail. A plaintiff must prove the existence and quantum (amount) of the loss for the court to award damages. In the English legal system there are several categories of damages.

- General damages are awarded for a loss that cannot be calculated, such as a personal injury.
- Special damages are awarded for a loss that can be calculated, such as lost salary during absence from work as a result of a personal injury.
- Liquidated damages are the specific amount calculated as the loss suffered, such as the precise sum required to compensate the loss suffered, or the sum described in the contract that has been breached.
- Unliquidated damages are not a fixed amount, but are left to the discretion of the court.
- Punitive (or exemplary) damages are awarded in addition to compensation for the loss suffered where the court seeks to punish the defendant or to demonstrate that the defendant's action was so deplorable that mere compensatory damages would not be sufficient to compensate the plaintiff.
- Nominal damages are a small amount awarded as a token to show that the loss suffered was not genuinely serious, such as an award of £1 as LIBEL damages.

In all its guises, damages looks at the concept of loss from every angle.

DEADLOCK COMPANY

A name given to a JOINT VENTURE company with a

corporate structure and constitution that require
unanimity among its shareholders before any significant action is taken which might affect their
interests in the company.

> *If that's justice, I'm a banana.*
> Ian Hislop, editor of *Private Eye*, after a jury in a libel case had
> awarded damages of £600,000 against the magazine

DEBENTURE
A formal acknowledgement by a company that it
owes a debt and that the debt is secured on the
assets of the company. It can be a document to
record a private debt or SECURITY arrangement
between a company and a lender, but a debenture
may also be used as a NEGOTIABLE INSTRUMENT – a
security that can be transferred from one holder to
another. If the debenture is one among several or
a series of debentures, it is known as debenture
stock with certificates (in a similar form to share
certificates) issued to holders (lenders). The rights
and powers of the debenture holders are set out
in a governing trust deed that is executed by the
company.

DEBT FINANCE
In MERGERS AND ACQUISITIONS parlance, debt finance
is an overblown name for a loan. In a VENTURE CAP-
ITAL transaction, it can be contrasted with EQUITY
CAPITAL. The equity provider invests for shares and
seeks its return from dividends and capital growth
of the shares. The DEBT PROVIDER invests by way of
a loan with provision for interest, a period for
repayment and usually some SECURITY. The debt
provider always gets its money back (provided
there is some) before the equity provider, as dividends can only be paid from distributable profits,
which are calculated after satisfaction of all relevant liabilities including interest due on debt. The
cost of debt finance (that is, the level of interest
that must be paid) is directly proportional to the
level of RISK assessed by the lender. If the borrower looks a safe bet or can provide attractive

security, the interest rates will be competitive. If not, they will not be (see MEZZANINE FINANCE).

DEBT PROVIDER

A lender or a bank providing DEBT FINANCE to a borrower, especially in a transaction involving VENTURE CAPITAL.

DEED

A legal document executed with all formality, that is, signed, sealed and delivered by the parties. Apart from the level of formality, there are two main distinctions between an agreement under SEAL (a deed) and an agreement under hand (a CONTRACT). First, an agreement under seal does not need the element of CONSIDERATION necessary for a mere contract to be valid and binding. Second, the LIMITATION PERIOD for an action arising from breach of a deed is extended to 12 years.

DEFAMATION

Defamation is a TORT. It is a wrong or injury to a living person's reputation or character, so that a right-thinking citizen may think less of him or her as a result of the wrong. If it is written down, the defamation is a LIBEL. If it is spoken, the defamation is a SLANDER. Different legal jurisdictions provide for different degrees of defamation. In the USA the tort is mollified by the First Amendment to the constitution, whereas in the UK there is no similar constitutional right to free speech (since it has no written constitution) and freedom of speech depends entirely on the principles of COMMON LAW. Similarly, different jurisdictions allow different defences to an alleged defamation, but the most common (and most interesting, since to succeed with it the DEFENDANT must justify the character assassination of the PLAINTIFF) is that the words were true. Examples are legendary and constantly fill the popular press; sex scandals and politicians have enduring appeal in the UK. Others are somewhat more unexpected. A British socialist politician complained of a defamation after a national newspaper questioned his working-class credentials. A TV star, famous for playing an ordinary character in a long-running soap opera, objected to being labelled boring and filed a defamation suit. Both were less than successful in their actions.

Apart from the scandal, the other interesting element of defamation is the amount of DAMAGES awarded to the victim. Although it is common for US juries to determine the amount of damages for a successful plaintiff in various types of LITIGATION, a defamation case is one of few cases in the UK where the JUDGE asks the JURY to decide on LIABILITY and then make the award. This has produced some startling results with massive awards, leading many legal commentators to conclude that mere jurors should not be trusted with anything as important as the law.

Judge Willis: *You are extremely offensive, young man.*
F.E. Smith: *As a matter of fact, we both are, and the only difference between us is that I am trying to be, and you can't help it.*
Judge Willis: *What do you suppose I am on the Bench for, Mr Smith?*
F.E. Smith: *It is not for me to attempt to fathom the inscrutable workings of Providence.*

DEFENDANT
A person who is sued in LITIGATION or one who is accused of an offence in criminal proceedings.

DE MINIMIS
An abbreviation of *de minimis non curat lex*, which means the law is not concerned with trivial matters – not, as has been suggested, the law does not care about the little people.

DEPOSITION
A written statement of evidence. In marked contrast to the English system, the US LITIGATION system relies heavily on pre-trial depositions. Each side's witnesses appear before the other side's

lawyers (with the comfort of their own lawyers to see fair play) to answer questions about the case, along the lines of DIRECT EXAMINATION. The answers are given under OATH and are recorded by a court official, so that the written transcript becomes part of the documents presented to the court at trial. It is intended to speed up the process by shortening the time required for taking evidence at the trial.

DEVELOPMENT CAPITAL
This is VENTURE CAPITAL invested in a business after it has established itself and needs more funds to expand its trading base. Most venture capital invested in a MANAGEMENT BUY-OUT and similar corporate financing is more accurately described as development capital because the business is invariably well established and less risky than a start-up operation (see SEED CAPITAL).

DEVISE
A gift of FREEHOLD land to someone under a WILL. A gift of other property is a BEQUEST or a LEGACY.

DIRECT EXAMINATION
The US term for EXAMINATION IN CHIEF.

DIRECTOR
The directors of a company are responsible for its management; they conduct and control its affairs and must answer to the owners (the MEMBERS) for its performance. Directors bear personal responsibility for carrying out their duties to the company and for ensuring that the company carries out its duties under the law. Since a company cannot go to prison for breaking the law, sometimes a director must go in its place. The law also recognises that some people wield the powers of directors without necessarily assuming the TITLE and seeks to hold them accountable as if they were directors (see SHADOW DIRECTOR). The procedure for the appointment and removal of a director is set out in a company's ARTICLES OF ASSOCIATION. (See also ALTERNATE DIRECTOR and NON-EXECUTIVE DIRECTOR.)

DISCOVERY

The formal, pre-trial disclosure by each party in LITIGATION of its written evidence. Discovery follows many and detailed rules of what must and must not be disclosed, with timetables and other procedural issues set by the court. In the USA the written evidence of each side's witnesses (see DEPOSITION) forms an important part of the discovery process.

DISCRETIONARY TRUST

For the basic meaning see TRUST. A discretionary trust, as opposed to a BARE TRUST, gives the trustee a discretion to select one of a number of potential beneficiaries to benefit from the trust fund. The class of beneficiaries, as the potential beneficiaries are known, are usually described in the trust deed or other foundation document. They can be as wide or as narrow as the creator of the trust (the SETTLOR) wishes. For example, a charitable trust will describe them in general terms, say, for the benefit of deaf people or for the education of the sons and daughters of poor people. Alternatively, a private (family) trust may give the trustees a discretion to favour one or more children of the settlor according to their needs or their good behaviour.

This latter type of discretionary trust is used extensively for tax-planning purposes around the world. The wealthy taxpayer (the settlor) gives (settles) a sum of money or property (the trust fund) to trustees on a discretionary trust whereby they have power to invest the trust fund and subsequently apply its income and/or capital for the benefit of a class of beneficiaries. The class will typically include one or two well-known charities, as well as (not surprisingly) the children of the settlor. The magic of the scheme for avoiding tax is that the trust fund no longer belongs to the wealthy taxpayer (who, as settlor, has given it away absolutely to the trustees and is carefully excluded from the class of beneficiaries). Nor does it belong to the trustees, who are merely holding it for the beneficiaries and are themselves carefully excluded from the class of beneficiaries. And, hey presto, it does not belong to the beneficiaries either because, under a discretionary trust, none of them has a right to call for any part of the trust fund; they each must wait to see in whose favour the trustees decide to exercise their discretionary powers. So until the discretion is exercised the taxman cannot say who owns the trust fund and should pay tax on it. Of course the taxman, as well as the wealthy taxpayer, has clever lawyers and around the world tax authorities have been closing these loopholes in the tax net. In the UK and the USA, for example, tax is levied on the trustees where they are resident within the tax jurisdiction. Hence the flight of trust funds to offshore trustees based in tax havens (Bermuda, the Channel Islands and so on). But such services are naturally expensive and this combination of competing forces means that only the wealthiest individuals can afford to avoid paying tax in their home jurisdiction.

A gentleman haranguing on the perfection of our law, and that it was equally open to the poor and the rich, was answered by another, "so is the London Tavern".
John Horne Tooke, 1794

DISSOLUTION

The ending of a marriage, a PARTNERSHIP, the life of a company or any other contractual venture by an administrative act or by the order of a court. A dissolution of a UK company occurs when the REGISTRAR OF COMPANIES strikes a company's name off the Companies' Register, usually for failing to comply with its regulatory responsibilities. The company can be restored to the register on the application of a creditor, so it does not provide an escape route for rogue directors and is not the same as a LIQUIDATION.

DISTRIBUTORSHIP

Where a distributor acquires goods, such as motor

cars, from a supplier or manufacturer with a view to selling them to its customers, it acquires TITLE to them and then sells them on its own account. In contrast, if the distributor were operating under an AGENCY arrangement, it would not acquire title but would merely sell them on behalf of the supplier (its PRINCIPAL). Although it is acting independently of the supplier, the distributor may be forced by the supplier to accept obligations and restrictions on its business practices as part of the supply agreement (especially if it is an EXCLUSIVE agreement). These obligations will be justified largely by the supplier's need to ensure that its trading reputation is maintained and protected, such as to provide for adequate after-sales servicing and repairs. Others may be less easy to justify, for example price fixing, and may be anti-competitive (see ANTI-TRUST). For a restrictive type of distributorship agreement see SOLUS AGREEMENT.

If he only knew a little of law, he would know a little of everything.
Anon

DUE DILIGENCE

Another US term that has found its way around the world in the jargon of MERGERS AND ACQUISITIONS lawyers. A due diligence investigation is a detailed review by a buyer or a potential buyer of the financial and other affairs of a TARGET COMPANY. This exercise can be carried out either before a CONTRACT is signed, or after a contract is signed but before COMPLETION or CLOSING, where its implications are agreed in the contract, usually as a price adjustment based on the findings of the investigation. This latter arrangement is used where the seller is reluctant to allow a potential buyer to crawl over its company, alarm its workforce and disrupt its smooth operations without giving a binding commitment to proceed with the acquisition.

E

EARN-OUT

A term used in MERGERS AND ACQUISITIONS to describe a price formula for the acquisition of a company based on its post-acquisition earnings. For example, the purchaser may agree to pay the seller 10% more than the basic purchase price if the business produces 10% more profits in the first year after the acquisition. An earn-out mechanism is usually included as an incentive for the company's management, who may have been the sellers of the company or otherwise involved in the acquisition transaction, to maintain their performance under the new owners.

EASEMENT

An ancient and archaic mechanism of COMMON LAW that is used, sometimes with difficulty, to cover a range of vital rights over land. These are private, not public, rights, which can be enjoyed only by the owner of the relevant land. They include a right of way over neighbouring land or a right not to be dwarfed by a neighbouring building (a right of light). Difficulties arise because of the technical limitations behind the concept of an easement. A true easement attaching to one piece of land (quaintly called the dominant tenement) must relate to another piece (the servient tenement) either adjoining or close by the dominant tenement. This requirement of proximity can cause problems. There may be good reasons for establishing an easement between two parcels of land some way apart, but when this concept was born in the Middle Ages no one looked further than the land just over their fence.

EIUSDEM GENERIS

Latin for "of the same kind". This expression is used to describe a rule of legal construction. If someone drawing up a document chooses a list of words ending in a word of general meaning, this rule will dictate that the general word should be construed with reference to the earlier, more specific words. For example, if the list refers to patents, trade marks, service marks and other rights, the reference to other rights will be interpreted to mean other INTELLECTUAL PROPERTY rights, not some wider meaning of indeterminable rights.

EMBLEMENTS

The law needs definitions for things that most people would not even think about. This is one. Emblements are vegetable and cereal products from agricultural cultivation of land. The definition is used where a landowner allows a farmer to use his land for a limited purpose, that being the taking of emblements. No grazing of cattle is allowed, just the taking of emblements. It is a good word and you should try using it at the supermarket.

EMOLUMENTS

A long but otherwise unremarkable word meaning all kinds of remuneration, such as salary, bonus, benefits and so on, received by employees from their employment.

Riches without law are more dangerous than is poverty without law.
Henry Ward Beecher, 1887

EMPLOYEE SHARE OWNERSHIP PLAN

An arrangement (such as a TRUST) used by a UK company to enable employees to acquire its shares over a number of years. There are many different structures for an employee share ownership plan (ESOP), and differing tax treatments depending on the structure, but generally the ESOP body (typically the trustee) acquires existing shares from shareholders or rights to new shares from the company and offers them for sale to the company's employees at preferential rates.

ENCUMBRANCE

A LIABILITY, such as a LIEN or a CHARGE, attaching to an asset or other property. If people sell property free of encumbrances, they are giving a WARRANTY that no one else has any claim over the property.

ENGROSSMENT

A legal document in its final form, ready for signature. In the good old days this would mean a script painstakingly written out on parchment by an ancient clerk with a quill pen. In more recent times the document would have been bound with green ribbon and carefully set to red-lined margins. Nowadays, if you are lucky, it is just word-processed and stapled.

EN VENTRE SA MERE

English law often turns to a foreign language to deal with a slightly delicate issue. In his mother's womb is an easy translation. The expression is used in wills and trusts to describe unborn children, alive and kicking but not yet in this world, who may fall within a class of beneficiaries. The TESTATOR or SETTLOR may wish the class to include those of his sons and daughters, and their own offspring, who are living or who are *en ventre sa mère* at the date of his death. Thus all the bases are covered.

E&OE

This is an abbreviation of errors and omissions excepted – an early form of EXCLUSION CLAUSE. No longer in widespread use, it was printed on the bottom of an invoice – before the days of minuscule and extensive terms and conditions printed on the reverse – to signify that the seller was reserving the right to amend its claim for payment if it discovered an error or omission at a later stage. All it signified was that the invoice should not be treated as the final word.

EQUAL OPPORTUNITIES

This is the implementation of a policy to remove discrimination in the workplace, including racial and sexual discrimination. With particular focus on equality between the sexes, an equal opportunities programme is intended to ensure that men and women have the same chances of employment, remuneration and career development. Some countries have gone one step further by allowing affirmative action, that is, discrimination in favour of groups that are considered to be disadvantaged.

EQUITY

As English law developed, it became apparent that strict adherence to the rules of precedent under COMMON LAW could, and often did, lead to injustice. To correct the balance, the courts gradually established a set of rules that could be applied in appropriate circumstances to override the rigid rules of precedent. These rules are known as the laws of equity. They are similar to the concept of GOOD FAITH found in CIVIL LAW, but they do not have the same universal application. For example, litigants can call on the principles of equity only if they can show unblemished conduct on their own part. Hence the unforgettable maxim that "he who comes to equity must come with clean hands".

Equity gives considerable discretion to the JUDGE, who must decide whether it is appropriate for equitable principles to prevail. It also gives the more creative judges an opportunity to manipulate the development of the law by sidestepping an unattractive precedent in reliance on some amorphous concept from equity. Generally, equity does not show its face in matters of commercial law, which for the sake of certainty depend so much on the application of firm legal principles. The human face of equity is best seen in family and matrimonial law, where, in the UK, property is divided among various claimants more often on grounds of need rather than strict legal ownership.

Wrong must not win by technicalities.
Aeschylus, 458 BC

EQUITY CAPITAL

Not to be confused with EQUITY as in the system of law, equity capital means an investment with an element of ownership in an asset; for example, a householder's equity in his house is that part not

---

pledged to a mortgagee. If an investor contributes equity capital to a company, it gets shares in the company and looks for its return through dividends paid on the shares or a rise in their capital value. An investor also has some say in the running of the company if the shares carry voting rights. This can be contrasted with a DEBT PROVIDER, which makes its investment by way of a loan with provision for interest, a period for repayment and usually some SECURITY, but has no ownership rights in the company. In the ranking of interests (that is, who gets paid first), debt always comes before equity.

ESCALATOR CLAUSE
Legal jargon meaning a provision in a CONTRACT whereby the price for the goods or services supplied will increase automatically on the occurrence of stated events or the passing of time.

ESCAPE CLAUSE
A provision in a CONTRACT that allows a party to avoid fulfilling its obligations without suffering a penalty. For example, a FORCE MAJEURE clause may operate as an escape clause.

ESCROW
Put on ice. If two parties sign a CONTRACT but do not want it come into effect until something else happens, they can hand it to a third party to hold until the condition is satisfied. This is holding the document in escrow; the instructions to the third party are contained in an escrow agreement; the third party is known as the escrow agent. Everything is frozen pending the fulfilment of the condition. If it happens as anticipated, the escrow agent must deliver up the document (and thereby consummate the contract) or face the consequences of breaching the escrow agreement. Neither of the contacting partners can stop the agent doing this; when the contract is signed and put in escrow, they bind themselves to the deal subject only to fulfilment of the specified condition. An escrow account is used to hold money until a

specified condition is satisfied, such as an exchange of contracts. In any escrow arrangement everyone must trust the escrow agent.

ESOP
See EMPLOYEE SHARE OWNERSHIP PLAN.

ESQUIRE
An example of two countries divided by a common language. In the UK esquire (usually abbreviated to Esq) is used as a formal title after the name of a man, but never a woman. It should be used only in addressing a letter to someone as in John Smith Esq, 42 Acacia Avenue, etc, and is an alternative (never an addition) to the title Mr. It is typically used by bank managers when they write politely to ask for their money back. In the USA, in contrast, it is used only as a title for a lawyer, either male or female.

ESTABLISHMENT (RIGHT OF)
One of the founding principles of the European Union, as embodied in the TREATY OF ROME, is that a citizen of a member state has the right to live and work in any other member state. This is the right of establishment. It is generally accepted but there are one or two problems, particularly over the right to work. For example, a worker may have the necessary qualifications to practise a profession in his or her home country but is rejected by a professional body in another member state because the qualifying requirements are different. It will take some time for these anomalies to be sorted out.

Lawyers are the people who rescue your estate from your enemies, and then keep it for themselves.
Henry Brougham

ESTATE
An interest in property (as in REAL ESTATE) or all the property owned by a person at the time of death (as in a deceased person's estate).

ESTOPPEL

One of the rules of EQUITY that overrides the potentially harsh impact of COMMON LAW. Estoppel prevents someone from denying something that he has lead another to believe or to rely on as an indisputable fact. It is an example of equity injecting an element of fairness into legal interpretation. Thus if a trader has habitually waived compliance with the strict terms of a contract during an extended course of dealing with another trader, he will be estopped from suddenly demanding strict compliance without giving reasonable notice. A handy tool such as this, used by the more adept judges, can avoid slavish devotion to precedent and sometimes can make all the difference between justice and injustice. (For more examples see PROMISSORY ESTOPPEL.)

ESTOVERS

Like EMBLEMENTS, this is a quaint expression of ancient COMMON LAW that probably could have been jettisoned some time ago. It refers to a tenant's right to take wood and timber from the land he leases. It is vital to someone, evidently.

EXAMINATION IN CHIEF

When a witness is in court being asked questions by the lawyer for his side so he can present his evidence, this questioning (the friendly questions) is known as the examination in chief (in the USA, the DIRECT EXAMINATION). Thereafter the witness will be asked questions by the lawyer for the other side (the unfriendly questions). This is the CROSS EXAMINATION.

We do not get good laws to restrain bad people.
We get good people to restrain bad laws.
G.K. Chesterton, 1908

EXCLUSION CLAUSE

A clause in a CONTRACT that seeks to exclude or limit the liability of one of the parties. Where a car park has a sign saying "All cars parked at the owner's risk", this is an exclusion clause seeking to exclude liability on the part of the car park operator. Similarly, a supplier of goods may seek to limit its liability to just replacing or repairing defective goods. In many jurisdictions the permissibility of an exclusion clause is restricted. In the UK the Unfair Contract Terms Act invalidates any exclusion clause to the extent that it seeks to exclude liability for death or personal injury. In other circumstances, particularly where the party concerned is a consumer, the act allows a court to strike out any exclusion clause it considers to be unreasonable.

EXCLUSIVE
An exclusive AGENCY or DISTRIBUTORSHIP agreement gives the agent or distributor the right to be the only person selling particular products in particular territories. This is a major benefit since the agent or distributor can rely on there being no competition for the products; if customers want them, they must buy them through the exclusive agency or distributorship. This, of course, excludes some competitive forces from the market and unsurprisingly exclusive agreements are the target of ANTI-TRUST LEGISLATION (see TREATY OF ROME). However, legislators recognise that sometimes exclusivity is necessary; for example, where a manufacturer cannot find an agent or distributor to handle its goods unless it offers exclusivity as a lure.

EX DIVIDEND
Where a SHARE is offered to a buyer ex dividend, it means the buyer will not be entitled to receive a recently declared dividend payment (which will go to the seller) and the sale price has been adjusted accordingly. In contrast, where a share is quoted CUM DIVIDEND, it will carry the right to receive the anticipated dividend.

EXECUTOR
The legal representative of a deceased person's ESTATE. An executor is appointed in a person's WILL to ensure that the terms of the will are carried out.

The appointment is confirmed by the granting of PROBATE.

EXEMPLARY DAMAGES
See PUNITIVE DAMAGES.

EX GRATIA
This Latin expression, meaning literally "as a favour", is used to describe the making of a gift, usually money, without any admission of LIABILITY on the part of the giver. It is useful because it allows the parties in a dispute to reach a settlement, involving the payment of money from one to the other, without anybody making a formal admission of guilt. The giver is pleased because he can tell the world that he made a settlement which did not involve the admission of liability. The recipient is pleased because he gets the money.

EX PARTE
Another Latin expression, meaning literally "on behalf of". Where an *ex parte* application is made to a court only one side in the dispute is represented and usually no notice is given to the other side; for example, where the application is for an INJUNCTION. The applicant must convince the JUDGE that there are pressing reasons for granting the injunction without hearing the other side. If the application is successful, the judge will invariably grant the order for only a short time and will require both parties to appear before the court within a matter of days to present the full story. The hearing is then INTER PARTES.

> *If there isn't a law, there will be.*
> Harold Faber, 1968

EXPERT WITNESS
A specialist in a particular field, such as a doctor or an accountant, who is brought before a court by a litigant to give evidence on technical issues. Inevitably, the other side will bring their own

expert witness to trump the evidence of the first witness, thereby leaving the court to decide on the correct interpretation from the competing arguments. This can be difficult in highly technical areas.

EXPRESS TERM

A written term of a CONTRACT. It is easier to prove but no more effective than an IMPLIED TERM.

FACTORING

A common technique for financing a trade that suffers from cash-flow difficulties. Factoring is the practice of selling your debts to a banker (the factor) as soon as they arise. The factor immediately pays you a percentage, say 80%, of the face value of the debts and thereafter collects payment from your customers on your behalf, keeping an agreed part as commission. This enables you to put the proceeds of your debts directly into your business without giving any credit period to your customers. There are disadvantages. You do not get 100% of your debts and your customers may not like the aggressive debt collection tactics of the factor.

FAIR DEALING

A defence to a claim of infringement of COPYRIGHT, fair dealing is quoting an extract from an article or other copyright work without the permission of the author for the purposes of analysis, criticism or news reporting. Convention requires that you should give an appropriate acknowledgement of the source of the extract and that the treatment of the extract must be fair.

FAIR MARKET VALUE

An objective assessment of the price a willing buyer would pay a willing seller for a particular asset, on the assumption that both buyer and seller are reasonably experienced in the particular market. It is often used as a formula in a CONTRACT to enable a third party, such as an arbitrator or a valuation expert, to set a fair price for a transaction (often to take place at some time in the future) between the contracting parties.

FALSE ACCOUNTING

The criminal offence of creating incorrect or misleading accounting records with a view to concealing an act of dishonesty. It is the final weapon in the armoury of the FRAUD prosecutor. Almost invariably when someone is facing charges of fraud or embezzlement, the last alleged offence on the charge sheet will be false accounting. When the DEFENDANT has been acquitted of all the other charges the prosecution's last chance of success will lie here, as a wrong entry is much easier to prove than the bigger crime of fraud.

You're an attorney. It's your duty to lie, conceal and distort everything, and slander everybody.
Jean Giraudoux, 1945

FAMILY DIVISION
One of the three divisions of the HIGH COURT, the Family Division deals with divorce, matrimonial property and children.

FEE SIMPLE
An ancient term, still used as a principle of land law, to mean an unrestricted freehold interest in REAL ESTATE.

FEE TAIL
Another expression aged for many years in oak casks, this is an interest in REAL ESTATE that can be passed only to the owner's direct descendants and will revert elsewhere if the line dies out. Similarly, a fee tail male can be passed only to male descendants. This is the stuff that novels such as Jane Austen's *Pride and Prejudice* are made of.

FIDUCIARY
Acting in the capacity of a TRUSTEE.

FIERI FACIAS
One of the better Latin expressions, meaning literally "make it happen" or perhaps "go for it". It is surprising it has not yet been used as an advertising slogan for a sports shoe company. It describes a court order, known as a WRIT of *fieri facias* or *fi.fa.*, ordering a court bailiff to seize the goods of a debtor to satisfy a judgement.

FIFTH AMENDMENT
The amendment to the US constitution which says

that individuals cannot be forced to give evidence that might incriminate them. By relying on this constitutional right, you can refuse to answer questions before a court or a tribunal. This right to silence, thought to be a fundamental principle of most legal systems, has recently been eroded in the UK where judges are now empowered to instruct juries that they may draw an adverse conclusion if defendants refuse to give evidence in their own trials.

FINAL JUDGEMENT
The judgement awarded at the end of a trial, as opposed to an INTERLOCUTORY judgement at an intermediate hearing.

> *The law is what it is – a majestic edifice, sheltering all of us, each stone of which rests on another.*
> John Galsworthy, 1910

FINANCE LEASE
A mechanism used by banks and lending institutions to make loans to enable borrowers to purchase assets (usually plant or equipment) whereby the bank retains an interest in the assets by way of SECURITY. Usually the lender retains ownership of the assets until all the loan has been repaid. The repayments are made as rent under the lease, with a further mechanism for the transfer of ownership (for example, by the payment of an additional sum) at the end of the lease period.

FINANCIAL ASSISTANCE
The COMPANIES ACTS restrict a company from providing financial assistance for the acquisition of its own shares. These rules were introduced in the UK (in the USA there are no such restrictions) to prevent the asset-stripping of companies. Unsentimental financiers and other wheeler-dealers were purchasing companies with finance raised on the SECURITY of the TARGET COMPANY's own assets, then promptly closing down its business and selling off

(stripping) the assets to repay their borrowings and turn a nice profit at the same time. The original rules against financial assistance were broadly drawn to restrict a wide range of activity. Recently the UK government has relaxed them, particularly for private companies, which may now dabble in this area provided that their MEMBERS give consent and the transaction does not affect the company's financial health. Nevertheless, it was probably these rules that saved the UK from the worst excesses of the leveraged transactions (see LEVER-AGED BUY-OUT) that plagued the USA in the late 1980s and led to the financing crises of the early 1990s.

FINANCIAL STATEMENTS

A company's accounts showing its financial position at the end of an accounting period. The financial statements include a balance sheet, profit and loss (income in the USA) statement and supporting notes. Save for exceptions allowed for smaller companies, every company must have its financial statements audited every year and then present them to its MEMBERS for approval at its annual GENERAL MEETING.

FIRM

A PARTNERSHIP or other unincorporated business. Although in common use, it is technically incorrect to refer to a limited company or other form of corporation as a firm.

FIRST INSTANCE

In LITIGATION, where a case is tried at first instance or heard by a court of first instance, it merely refers to the court in which the case was first tried before going on APPEAL to a higher court.

FITNESS FOR PURPOSE

Often an IMPLIED TERM in a CONTRACT for the sale of goods. In the UK it is implied by the SALE OF GOODS ACTS, but it can be excluded by agreement between the parties. It implies a WARRANTY by the seller that the goods will be fit for the purpose for which they are commonly expected to be used. If not, the buyer may have a claim for DAMAGES against the seller.

> *"If the law supposes that,"* said Mr Bumble, *"the law is a ass – a idiot."*
> Charles Dickens, *Oliver Twist*

FIXED ASSETS

The assets owned by a company that form part of its business infrastructure rather than those (current) assets that it sells to customers as goods or uses up in producing its goods. Typically, fixed assets include FREEHOLD REAL ESTATE, plant and machinery.

FIXED CHARGE

A MORTGAGE or other SECURITY given by a company that attaches to specified assets (such as REAL ESTATE) in order to prevent their disposal without satisfying the interest of the person holding the charge (the chargee). In contrast, see FLOATING CHARGE.

FLOATING CHARGE

A MORTGAGE or other SECURITY taken on a company's assets as they flow in and out as part of its trading operations. In contrast to a FIXED CHARGE, which attaches to specific assets (such as REAL ESTATE) and prevents their disposal, a floating charge floats on the top of (or, perhaps, hovers above) specified categories of assets (such as work-in-progress or inventory) and attaches only to the specific assets within those categories in the event of default (for example, the borrower failing to make a repayment or otherwise breaching its loan obligations). This allows the company to give security over its trading assets but to retain the freedom to use them for its normal business operations. If it suffers a default, the security crystallises and the charge becomes fixed on the relevant assets owned by the company at that moment.

FLOTATION

The offering of shares (or other securities) in a company to the public on a stock exchange. In the UK a defining characteristic of a PRIVATE COMPANY is that it cannot offer its shares to the public. This is the exclusive realm of a PUBLIC COMPANY. When a public company allows its shares to be added to the stock exchange's list of shares available for buying and selling by the public, it becomes a LISTED COMPANY. Its shares are then valued by the market forces of independent buyers and sellers and its overall value (MARKET CAPITALISATION) moves up and down with the market. Hence the expression that a company has floated its shares on a stockmarket.

FOB

The acronym for free on board, a term used in international trade contracts for the supply of goods to determine when the RISK in the goods passes from the seller to the buyer. Under an FOB contract the seller agrees to deliver the goods to a ship at a specified port at its own cost and risk. When the goods have crossed the ship's rail, they become the responsibility of the buyer. There is a marvellous case where the court had to decide who bore the risk when a large piece of machinery fell from the crane on to the ship's rail before plunging to the depths of the sea. (For another example of abbreviated trade terms see CIF.)

FORCE MAJEURE

An intervening event, beyond the control of the parties, which prevents a CONTRACT from being performed. The favourite example is an act of God (which is a brave concept in the field of legal interpretation) where, for example, a storm blows a ship off course and prevents the shipper from delivering its consignment of beans to Genoa on or before Michaelmas day. Where a contract includes a force majeure clause, the shipper cannot be sued for breach of contract in so far as the breach resulted from the force majeure event. The trick in drafting the clause, from the viewpoint of the performing party, is to define the scope of the force majeure event as widely as possible. For example, it might reasonably cover war, terrorist activities and acts of God, but it might also include strikes or other industrial disputes (an imprecise concept) or even something as uncertain as transport delays. The widest event, which is commonly found in these clauses, is "any event beyond the reasonable control of the performing party". This provides broad scope for a massive argument before anyone admits LIABILITY.

What is the difference between an attorney and God?
God doesn't think he's an attorney.
Anon

FORECLOSE
To take possession of property covered by a MORTGAGE or other SECURITY, usually for the purpose of selling it, because the owner has defaulted on the loan for which the property was charged. The person making the foreclosure (the mortgagee) is entitled to set off the proceeds of sale of the property against the outstanding loan but must return any surplus to the owner.

FRANCHISE
A right, in the form of a LICENCE granted in return for a ROYALTY, to use a brand name, "get-up" (representation or style of a business) and other collected property rights of a particular business in order to duplicate the business in another location and trade under the brand name. Famous name restaurant chains use this technique to extend their geographic scope without carrying the full investment burden. The franchisee provides the premises, hires the staff and runs the business; the franchiser provides the KNOW-HOW, often supplies the raw produce on an EXCLUSIVE basis and collects a royalty based on sales revenue.

Fraud

The basic meaning of fraud is a crime, a version of theft, whereby one person dishonestly obtains money or some other advantage from another by leading him to believe something to be true that is not. In English law the crime is ponderously described as "obtaining a pecuniary advantage by deception". Fraud also has a wider meaning, which covers a range of dishonest conduct along the lines of cheating. A fraudulent MISREPRESENTATION is a false statement intended to trick someone into entering into a CONTRACT. A fraudulent CONVEYANCE is a transfer of property to someone in order to prevent it being seized by creditors. Fraudulent trading is allowing a company to continue in business knowing that it is unlikely to be able to pay its debts. In this wider sense, the word is used as a qualifier to judge the standard of conduct of the perpetrator. Thus the consequences are more severe for fraudulent misrepresentation than for innocent misrepresentation.

Freehold

The absolute, unfettered right of ownership of land (see FEE SIMPLE).

Friendly society

A type of organisation that became popular in the UK in the 19th century and still survives today. A friendly society is a MUTUAL COMPANY. Members make regular contributions to establish a central fund, from which funds can be advanced to them for specified purposes, such as a pension or in the event of sickness.

Frustration

The doctrine of frustration (yes, it is a doctrine rather than an experience) is where one of the parties to a CONTRACT claims it cannot perform its obligation because of some intervening or frustrating event. For example, if you buy a ticket for a boxing match which is cancelled because one of the fighters is ill, the promoter might well invoke the doctrine of frustration in returning your ticket money to you.

FUNCTUS OFFICIO

Having shot one's bolt; spent; no longer wielding any power because you have already exercised it. For example, a JUDGE may be *functus officio* because he has given his judgement and no longer has any jurisdiction over the case.

It's perfectly obvious that somebody's responsible and somebody's innocent. Otherwise justice makes no sense at all.
Uto Betti, 1936

FUNGIBLES

A wonderful word referring to goods that can be measured by being counted, such as nuts in a bag, hay bales in a stack (but not loose hay), and rivets in a box. The possibilities are boundless and someone should invent a family board game based on it.

GAGGING ORDER

A term used more by journalists than lawyers, it refers to an INJUNCTION ordered by a court to restrain the publication of specified material in the press, in a book or otherwise. One of the most celebrated cases on this subject in recent times was the *Spycatcher* case, where the UK government sought an order to prevent the publication of a book of memoirs by a former secret service agent on the grounds that it would compromise national security.

GAMING

A typically dour, legalistic word to describe one of life's great pleasures, for some people at least. It is the playing of games of chance for money. In most countries you need a LICENCE to run it as a business, so that the government can tax you heavily. In some jurisdictions it is illegal.

Law-making is finding out what people enjoy doing most and either stopping them doing it or taxing them for it.

Anon

GARNISHEE ORDER

Where a creditor obtains a judgement against a debtor, who is owed money by someone else, the creditor can apply to the court for an order that the second debtor (the garnishee) must pay the money direct to him. Thus a garnishee order makes a debtor pay a creditor of his creditor, not his creditor himself, if you see what I mean.

GAZUMP

This is the practice of a seller informally agreeing terms for the sale of property, usually REAL ESTATE, but withdrawing and selling to another buyer at a higher price before the deal is formalised in a binding CONTRACT. In England and Wales (but not SCOTLAND) it is common practice for a buyer and seller of a house to agree terms SUBJECT TO CONTRACT. This means that, although they have agreed the terms, neither is contractually bound until a formal contract is signed and exchanged. This is intended to give both parties some time to get organised for the transaction to be formalised, but it leaves the buyer at risk of being gazumped.

GEARING

Known in the USA as leverage, this is the ratio of DEBT FINANCE to EQUITY CAPITAL in a company's capital structure. The distinction can become blurred by the introduction of intermediate forms of finance, such as loans that can be converted into shares when specific events take place. These types of financial instruments allow accountants to be creative when describing a company's gearing. A variety of formulae can be applied, all under the umbrella of gearing, to analyse the balance between debt and equity.

GENERAL MEETING

A meeting of the MEMBERS of a company. An annual general meeting (AGM) must be held every year for the members to consider the accounts (FINANCIAL STATEMENTS) and the report of the directors for the previous financial year. Other ordinary business at an AGM includes the declaration of any dividend, the appointment of auditors and the authority for the directors to determine the remuneration of the auditors. A general meeting other than an AGM is known as an extraordinary general meeting (EGM), which may be convened by the board of directors or on the requisition of a sufficient number of members. The necessary procedures for conducting general meetings of UK companies are set out in the COMPANIES ACTS and are supplemented by the provisions of a company's ARTICLES OF ASSOCIATION. General meetings provide the only formal occasion when the managers of a company (the directors) face the owners of the company (the members).

GENERAL NOTARY

See NOTARY PUBLIC.

GENTLEMEN'S AGREEMENT

An agreement that is not legally enforceable because there is no evidence to show that the parties intended to be legally bound at the time they made the contract. The distinction between a gentlemen's agreement and a CONTRACT can be fine and there is much CASE LAW on the subject. The theory behind a gentlemen's agreement is that true gentlemen will honour their obligations, even though they cannot be legally compelled to do so. Presumably this is to be contrasted with a businessmen's agreement.

GOOD FAITH

Some lawyers have difficulty with this, but it merely implies a general duty to act reasonably and honestly. Jurisdictions based on CIVIL LAW impose an underlying duty on all parties in transactions to act in good faith and will penalise any who do not. COMMON LAW jurisdictions impose no such burden and, apart from specific duties or matters of illegality, tend to avoid making moralistic judgements on a person's conduct.

We expect the law to be ideal and almost inspired, whereas it is only an imperfect, rough-and-ready device of mankind to keep people from sending each other to the devil.
George Bernard Shaw

GOODWILL

It is difficult to give a precise definition as it means something different in different contexts. Goodwill has one meaning for an accountant, another for a MERGERS AND ACQUISITIONS lawyer, and yet another for an INTELLECTUAL PROPERTY lawyer. It is an intangible asset, but since this only means you cannot touch it, it is not really helpful. At least it can be identified as an asset, although with its attendant accounting complexities it can sometimes look like a LIABILITY. At its simplest, goodwill refers to the value of the reputation attached to a trading asset. It can be the value of the clientele who frequent a restaurant. It can be the value of a brand name of a chocolate bar. It can be the value of a whole business after subtracting the value of its tangible assets (those you can touch). By virtue of their abstract nature, the assessment of these values is difficult and this is the start of the accounting problems. Accounting standards (see STATEMENT OF STANDARD ACCOUNTING PRACTICE) around the world lay down rules for how a company is required to treat goodwill in its FINANCIAL STATEMENTS. There is much international variation. The aim is to allow a company to reflect goodwill as an asset in its accounts where there is a genuine and identifiable value attaching to it, but not otherwise. The complexity of the accounting rules, however, can make this difficult to understand in practice.

GRAND JURY
A legal mechanism used at the start of US criminal proceedings. A JURY is presented with preliminary evidence against the accused and is asked to decide whether there are sufficient grounds to issue an INDICTMENT, which will take the matter to a full trial. Unlike a trial jury of 12, a grand jury can have up to 24 jurors.

GRAY'S INN
One of the four INNS OF COURT.

GREEN BOOK
The book of procedural rules of the County Courts of England and Wales.

GREEN FORM
A registration form used in the UK as a preliminary application for LEGAL AID, whereby a person can ask for free or subsidised advice from a SOLICITOR.

GROSS NEGLIGENCE
A serious breach of a duty to another person. This term is used to emphasise the severity of the circumstances surrounding a case of NEGLIGENCE.

GUARANTEE

A promise that something will happen. A guarantee by a manufacturer of goods is a promise to a purchaser that the goods will work as intended for the period of the guarantee; if not, the manufacturer will repair or replace the goods free of charge. In this sense the guarantee is a form of WARRANTY. To guarantee a debt is to promise that it will be paid in accordance with its terms. To guarantee the debt of another person is to promise that the person will pay the debt in accordance with its terms; if not, the guarantor will become directly liable for making the payment. In this sense the guarantee is a form of SECURITY.

Agree, for the law is costly.
W. Camden, 1614

GUARDIAN

A person appointed by law to represent and act on behalf of another, such as a MINOR, who cannot act on his or her own behalf.

H

HABEAS CORPUS
"Let him have his body back!" This is not an accurate translation, but it goes some way to explain this emotive slogan for the remedy against unlawful imprisonment. Civilised legal systems have rules that entitle the authorities to detain you for only a short time before formally charging you with an offence and bringing you before a court to answer the charge. If they hold you beyond the designated time, you can apply for a writ of habeas corpus and ask for your body back.

HABENDUM
A fairly pointless bit of Latin used as a name (if a name were needed) for the part of a CONVEYANCE of REAL ESTATE that describes how the property is to be transferred to the transferee. Conveniently, it usually starts with the words TO HOLD (the more considerate conveyancers have them typed in upper case for ease of identification). Many purchasers of real estate are blissfully unaware that their legal rights depend on a habendum.

HEARSAY EVIDENCE
If you are a witness at a trial and give evidence as to what someone told you had happened, rather than what you saw with your own eyes, it is hearsay and may be INADMISSIBLE EVIDENCE. The general rule is that witnesses should to give evidence on what they actually saw happen. In the UK the hearsay rule has recently been modified and hearsay evidence is admissable, but it may carry little weight.

HEREDITAMENT
An ugly word that should have been despatched into oblivion long ago. It refers generally to property that is capable of transfer from one person to another and particularly to REAL ESTATE. Corporeal hereditaments are tangible property such as buildings; incorporeal hereditaments are intangible property such as rights of way.

H

HEREIN

A favourite word of pompous people who draw
up documents. It merely means in this document,
but it can be used to great effect – particularly as
hereinafter, hereinbefore and so on – in making a
sentence sound more important than it is.

HIGH COURT

The High Court of Justice is the main civil court in
England and Wales. It is divided into three divisions, the QUEEN'S BENCH DIVISION, the CHANCERY
DIVISION and the FAMILY DIVISION, which deal with
claims in their own specialist areas. The High
Court hears all civil claims where the amount in
dispute exceeds £50,000 (the limit is increased
periodically). Smaller claims are heard by the
COUNTY COURT.

*The law is not what the court said last time, it is
what the court will say the next time.*
Mr Justice Blunt, 1946

HILARY

The Hilary term is one of the four terms in the
year for sittings of the courts in England and
Wales.

HIRE PURCHASE

Known in the USA as an instalment plan, a hire
purchase agreement allows you to purchase an
item by making payments over a period of time.
Typically, the RISK in the asset passes to the buyer
on delivery, but TITLE does not pass until payment
of the last instalment. This entitles the seller to
repossess the asset if the purchase price is not
paid.

HIVE DOWN

The transfer of assets from a company to a subsidiary company, often newly formed for this purpose, in order to separate (hive down or hive off)
one business from another. This is usually one
step in a corporate reorganisation, such as the

restructuring of a group or the sale of a business as a new unit.

HIVE UP

A similar transaction to a HIVE DOWN, except the assets are transferred from a company to its parent company rather than its subsidiary.

HOLDING COMPANY

A company that exists solely to hold shares in subsidiary companies and accordingly is not a trading company.

HOLDING OVER

If you occupy REAL ESTATE under a LEASE, and continue to occupy it after the lease has expired, you are said to be holding over on the same terms as set out in the lease.

HYPOTHECATE

A type of equitable MORTGAGE whereby you hand over possession of an asset as SECURITY for a debt, but you do not transfer TITLE or ownership of the asset (as you do with a legal mortgage).

IGNORANTIA LEGIS NON EXCUSAT

An expression that may be quoted by police officers with a classical education. Ignorance of the law is not an excuse. If you break the law you cannot claim as a defence that you did not know your action was illegal.

IMPEACHMENT

Originally used as a charge of treason made before PARLIAMENT, with the accused being marched off to the Tower of London without further ado. Impeachment has now been refined to mean a charge of misconduct against a head of state or (particularly in the USA) against any public official.

I am not a crook.
Richard Nixon, former president of the USA

IMPLIED TERM

A term of a CONTRACT that, although not written into the contract (which would have made it an EXPRESS TERM), a court will recognise as being part of the contractual relations between the parties. The most common is a term implied by STATUTE. In a contract for the sale of goods, for example, the SALE OF GOODS ACTS will impose certain terms on the seller (for example, regarding TITLE and MERCHANTABLE QUALITY), which will be implied in the contract even if they are not expressly stated. Apart from statutory implied terms, a court will sometimes find a reason to impose a term in a contract. It will not take this step lightly and there are rigid rules to govern when it should. For example, a court may correct a manifest error by implying a term without which the contract would not make sense – perhaps a price clause in a supply contract. A court will also recognise an implied term that has arisen from a course of dealing between the parties. A provision in an earlier contract is not always a guide to the current terms, but some provisions have the nature of continuity which a court may recognise.

IMPOSSIBILITY OF PERFORMANCE
Similar to the doctrine of FRUSTRATION, this is finding yourself in a position, as a party to a CONTRACT, where it is impossible to perform your obligations. You have contracted to sell your priceless Ming vase but your husband just dropped it. It does not mean you escape LIABILITY, but it puts an end to the doubt over whether you will perform or not.

INADMISSIBLE EVIDENCE
In LITIGATION the rules of play are long and often tedious, and in books that describe them many pages are taken up by the rules of evidence. What you can and what you cannot bring before the court is often a crucial issue in the outcome of a case. When something is ruled out it is said to be inadmissible, for example, HEARSAY EVIDENCE.

IN CAMERA
Inside a room where those not involved in the matter are not allowed; in private; without the public being present.

IN CHAMBERS
Next door to IN CAMERA. When a JUDGE hears a case or part of a case in chambers, it is heard in private without the public or the JURY (if there is one) being present. The lawyers are there, of course, because it is difficult to keep them out of the action.

INCHOATE
Incomplete or unfinished. An inchoate offence is one where the offending act was not completed but is nonetheless an offence; for example, attempted murder or CONSPIRACY.

INCITEMENT
Encouraging someone to carry out a crime; for example, incitement to cause racial hatred.

INCORPORATION
The act of forming a company by registering the appropriate documents with the appropriate regu-

latory authorities, which in the UK is the REGISTRAR OF COMPANIES and in the USA is the secretary of state of the selected jurisdiction. In the UK a company is not incorporated until the registrar issues the certificate of incorporation, which bears the company's official name, a registration number (which remains constant even if the company changes its name) and the date of incorporation.

> *No man is above the law and no man is below it;*
> *nor do we ask any man's permission when we*
> *ask him to obey it.*
> Theodore Roosevelt, 1904

INCORPOREAL HEREDITAMENT
A fancy expression for an intangible right (such as COPYRIGHT or a TRADE MARK) that can be passed from one person to another through inheritance.

INDEFEASIBLE RIGHT
A right that cannot be overturned or made void.

INDEMNITY
An acknowledgement of LIABILITY to pay someone compensation for a loss, if one occurs. The liability is absolute and unqualified. This means that the injured party is entitled to recover full compensation for the loss suffered, without any duty to mitigate the loss (in contrast to DAMAGES for breach of CONTRACT).

INDENTURE
An archaic word for a DEED. Also, in the past, it referred to the CONTRACT of apprenticeship whereby a trainee craftsman worked for a master craftsman for a designated time in order to learn a trade, as in articles of indenture or simply indentures. Originally, an indenture was written in duplicate on the same parchment, which on signature was torn apart so that each party retained one half. They could prove that the document was genuine by matching the two torn halves.

INDEPENDENT CONTRACTOR
A freelancer; a person carrying out services for another but not as an employee. If you are told what to do, but not how to do it, then you are an independent contractor. If you are told what to do and how to do it, then either you are married or you are an employee.

INDICTMENT
In the USA an indictment is the list of charges presented to a GRAND JURY for it to determine whether there is sufficient evidence for the accused to stand trial on those charges. In the UK it is the written statement presented to the CROWN COURT setting out the details of the crime with which the DEFENDANT is charged.

It ain't no sin if you crack a few laws now and then, just so long as you don't break any.
Mae West, 1937

INDIVIDUAL VOLUNTARY ARRANGEMENT
See SCHEME OF ARRANGEMENT.

INDUCEMENT
As a TORT, and therefore actionable by the person who suffers DAMAGES as a result, inducement to cause a breach of CONTRACT can have far-reaching implications. It has been used, for example, in industrial relations disputes to stop secondary picketing where an employer seeks to prevent striking workers from encouraging its suppliers to withhold supplies (and thereby break their contracts with the employer).

IN FLAGRANTE DELICTO
This Latin expression seems to have developed a sexual connotation, but it only means "in the act of committing a crime".

INJUNCTION
A court order compelling someone not to do something or to stop doing it because it infringes

someone else's rights. There are many examples: to stop the publication of a book containing information that might be a threat to national security (as in the *Spycatcher* case), or to stop the continuing infringement of a TRADE MARK or a PATENT. An interim injunction stops someone doing something during the course of LITIGATION until the case is heard at a full trial. A breach of an injunction is a CONTEMPT OF COURT.

INNER TEMPLE
One of the four INNS OF COURT.

INNS OF COURT
Every BARRISTER has to be a member of one of the four inns of court, which are Gray's Inn, Lincoln's Inn, Inner Temple and Middle Temple. The inns are situated close together on the western edge of the City of London. Each one has a few acres of land and comprises the barristers' SET OF CHAMBERS, usually positioned around courtyards or immaculate lawns. Barristers can have their chambers outside the inns, for example where they are based in other towns or cities, but every barrister must be a member of an inn and pay allegiance to its rules and regulations.

INQUEST
A formal investigation by a court, under the direction of a CORONER, into a person's death. An inquest has to be held where a death has occurred in unusual circumstances or may have resulted from someone's wrongdoing. Its primary task is to identify who died, when, where and what of. It will then look at the circumstances surrounding the death – for example, whether it was a pure accident or an unlawful killing. It is not part of its function to identify the killer. As an extraordinary addition to its scope of work, an inquest is also held to determine whether or not a find constitutes TREASURE TROVE.

INQUISITORIAL PROCEDURE
In countries such as most in continental Europe

that rely on the CIVIL CODE, the task of investigating crimes and conducting proceedings against alleged offenders is given to a MAGISTRATE or public official. The magistrate is responsible for bringing the necessary evidence before a court and is empowered to ask questions (hence inquisitorial) which must be answered. In contrast, COMMON LAW jurisdictions use the ACCUSATORIAL PROCEDURE where the prosecution (representing the state) presents the evidence and accuses the DEFENDANT of the alleged wrongdoing.

> *Laws are like spiders' webs which, if anything small falls into them they ensnare it, but large things break through and escape.*
> Solon, 600 BC

INQUORATE
A meeting that does not have the necessary QUORUM (number of people) and accordingly has no official standing.

IN RE
The Latin for "in the matter of". It is used as a TITLE for a court case where the court is asked to determine circumstances surrounding a specified person or legal entity, as in *In re Joe Smith* or *In re J. Smith & Co Ltd.*

INSIDER DEALING
The buying or selling of a company's securities by a person who has valuable knowledge that the general public does not have about the company's financial position. Although generally recognised as undesirable, some jurisdictions treat insider dealing as a crime whereas others leave it to be regulated under professional rules by the supervisory body of the stock exchange. The big problem is drawing an appropriate line between what is allowable and what is not. Most professional investors take investment decisions based on knowledge that they would like to think is ahead of the market. Making a decision or a shrewd

guess from generally available information can sometimes look like insider dealing. Since the rules are really intended to protect unwary investors, it has been suggested by an off-beat commentator (not entirely in jest) that the law should prohibit outsider dealing, not insider dealing, on the basis that investors should not be risking their money unless they have, or think they have, some special knowledge about the proposed investment.

INSTRUMENT
An obstruse word to describe a legal document, used only by lawyers seeking to confuse their clients.

INSURABLE INTEREST
To enter into a valid insurance CONTRACT, you have to be able to show that you have an interest in the asset you are seeking to insure. This means you either own it or would have a LIABILITY to someone if it were lost or damaged. Without this insurable interest you cannot make such a contract.

INTELLECTUAL PROPERTY
Clever property? More like property of the mind. This is a generic term to describe the family of ownership rights over an intangible asset such as a PATENT, TRADE MARK or COPYRIGHT.

"Write that down," said the king to the jury, and the jury eagerly wrote down all three dates on their slates and then added them up, and reduced the answer to shillings and pence.
Lewis Carroll, *Alice in Wonderland*

INTER ALIA
Latin for "among other things".

INTERDICT
A court order in SCOTLAND prohibiting someone from doing or continuing to do something (see INJUNCTION).

I

INTERIM
Not final; temporary. An interim INJUNCTION or an interim order is issued by a court during the INTERLOCUTORY proceedings leading up to a trial.

INTERLOCUTORY
A court hearing that takes place in preparation for a full trial, either so that a JUDGE may give instructions for the conduct of the trial or as an application for an INTERIM remedy, which may be confirmed or terminated at the full trial.

INTERNAL RATE OF RETURN
The fundamental creed of investment bankers and especially venture capitalists. In simple terms, the internal rate of return (IRR) is the compound annual rate of return on an investment. For a potential investor in a company it includes dividend distributions and discernible capital growth in the value of the shares. All venture capitalists have their own formulae for calculating the IRR and will argue about which items should be adjusted or written off in making the calculation. This means that few formulae produce the same result.

INTERNATIONAL BAR ASSOCIATION
An organisation of lawyers from around the world who meet periodically at exotic locations to promote a better understanding of international legal affairs and to have a good time.

INTERNATIONAL COURT OF JUSTICE
The court of the United Nations that sits in The Hague, Netherlands.

INTERNATIONAL LAW
Since there is no global legislature, there are no laws of universal application. International law derives its validity from inter-country treaties, which are nothing more than a form of CONTRACT, whereby one country agrees to bind itself and its citizens to an agreed course of conduct for the benefit of another country. These treaties are

often multinational, with a number of countries agreeing to be bound by them (as in the constitution of the United Nations or the international conventions governing reciprocal recognition of trade marks) for the benefit of each other. The structure of international trade is based on multinational treaties and conventions, which deal with tariffs, anti-competitive practices, INTELLECTUAL PROPERTY rights, finance and banking, taxation and so on.

INTER PARTES
Latin for "between the parties". It refers to a court hearing at which both sides are present, as opposed to an *ex parte* hearing when only one side usually attends.

INTER VIVOS
Latin for "between living people". It refers to a gift given by one living person to another, as opposed to a BEQUEST or a LEGACY, which is given by a person on his or her death.

> *Our nation is founded on the principle that observance of the law is the eternal safeguard of liberty and defiance of the law is the surest road to tyranny.*
> John F. Kennedy, 1962

INTESTATE
To die intestate means to die without making a valid WILL, whereupon the law determines that your ESTATE will be distributed to any surviving partner and children or, if there are none, to a prescribed list of close relatives. In the UK, if there is no one to collect at all, the property is given to the Crown (in other words the state) as BONA VACANTIA (vacant goods).

INTRA VIRES
Latin for "within the permitted powers". It refers to a public official acting on appropriate authority or a company engaging in dealings that are autho-

rised by its MEMORANDUM OF ASSOCIATION, as opposed to ULTRA VIRES, which means outside or beyond the permitted powers.

IOU
I owe you. A piece of paper that simply acknow-ledges the existence of a debt between one person and another. If asked to draft one, a lawyer would call it an unconditional, negotiable loan INSTRU-MENT and it would probably spread over 30 pages.

IPSO FACTO
Latin for "by the very fact itself". The existence of a certain fact that is sufficient to establish an alleged fact, as in traces of milk on the cat's whiskers.

IRR
See INTERNAL RATE OF RETURN.

ISSUED CAPITAL
The part of a company's NOMINAL CAPITAL that is for the time being issued to its MEMBERS. For example, a company may have a nominal capital of £10,000 divided into 10,000 shares of £1 each, but if it has issued only 5,000 shares its issued capital is £5,000.

JOINDER

An inelegant word used in LITIGATION to refer to the bringing together of several issues, several parties or several actions into a single action to be dealt with by a single court.

JOINT LIABILITY

A group of people with joint LIABILITY are liable as a group and their creditors must sue all of them together for the liability of the group. A group of people with SEVERAL LIABILITY are liable separately as individuals so their creditors must sue them individually only for the liability incurred by each of them. A group of people with joint and several liability are in the soup because they are liable both together as a group and separately as individuals. This means their creditors may sue any one of them or all of them for the liability of the whole group. A partner has joint and several liability for the debts of the PARTNERSHIP.

JOINT TENANCY

In contrast to a TENANCY IN COMMON, a joint tenancy is where two or more people hold an interest in a property together, not separately. They cannot deal with or dispose of the property without acting together. Also, if one of them dies, his or her interest is automatically transferred to the surviving joint tenant or tenant(s). This is called the right of survivorship. To break up a joint tenancy and turn it into a tenancy in common, see SEVERANCE.

The more laws, the less justice.
German proverb

JOINTURE

In some circles, when you get married, you enter into a marriage settlement or pre-nuptial agreement with your beloved in order to work out one or two distasteful issues over ownership of property in case you subsequently decide to go your separate ways. As a sweetener, and just to show it is nothing personal, you might make a gift or a

SETTLEMENT to your spouse as part of the deal. The assets that make up the gift or settlement are known as jointure.

JOINT VENTURE

A combination of two or more persons (either individuals or companies) for an agreed business purpose. The parties may choose to incorporate a new legal entity (a joint-venture company) to represent their interests; or they may operate as a PARTNERSHIP; or they may institute a less formal arrangement such as a co-operation agreement whereby they assume contractual obligations to each other short of a partnership. A corporate joint venture may have a complex capital structure, often with different classes of shares representing the different interests, each weighted with veto powers to ensure unanimity between the ventures on important issues. Where the veto powers are so extensive that no party can take any significant action without the support of the other parties, the company is known as a DEADLOCK COMPANY.

JUDGE

The one in the big wig? Not necessarily. In UK courts the judge will wear a wig, but only the more senior judges wear the long wig imagined in story books. Elsewhere around the world the judge usually gets a gown, a sash or something to remind everyone who is in charge, but he or she only wears these trappings in the courtroom when formal business is under way. Other duties occur outside the courtroom. A hearing in chambers (without the gear) means a less formal hearing in the judge's private room without the public or the JURY (if there is one). There are different categories of judge. A recorder is a BARRISTER or SOLICITOR who sits as a part-time judge while continuing to practise at the same time, often as a precursor to becoming a full time judge. A MASTER is a judge or a court official who hears preliminary issues in a case on its way to trial. In the UK all judges are appointed by the monarch on the recommendation of the LORD CHANCELLOR. There is a minimum requirement that they should have been a barrister or a solicitor of at least ten years' standing. Most will have been barristers, although there is a drive to appoint more solicitors. In the USA state judges are appointed by the state governor or elected in a general poll. Federal judges and SUPREME COURT judges are appointed by the president.

> *Trial by jury itself, instead of being a security to persons who are accused, will be a delusion, a mockery and a snare.*
> Lord Thomas Denman, 1844

JUDICIAL REVIEW

An important weapon in ADMINISTRATIVE LAW, judicial review is the examination by a court of an administrative decision to determine whether the decision has been made properly. In many cases the examination focuses on the powers of the person who made the decision or the decision-making process, rather than the correctness of the decision itself. For example, LEGISLATION may grant a discretion to a government minister to decide a policy for sentencing convicted murderers. No one can challenge the minister's decision if he has exercised his discretion properly, but a judicial review can examine whether or not he took into account all the relevant issues in exercising that discretion. Thus the review looks at the form of the decision-making process in an attempt to ensure that the substance of the decision has been reached in accordance with the law. Judicial review is loved by interventionist judges and hated by government ministers in a hurry.

JUNIOR

In a complex UK court case each side will traditionally have two barristers: a LEADER and a junior. The leader is the senior BARRISTER who leads the case. The junior plays a supporting role, researching the law, analysing the evidence, making suggestions and occasionally examining a witness. If the case is less complex, the junior may appear without a leader and conduct the case alone. As a departure from tradition and to save costs, it is now possible (and increasingly common) for a leader to appear without a junior.

JUNIOR DEBT

A loan by a borrower that ranks behind another loan, known as the SENIOR DEBT. Ranking or priority or SUBORDINATION indicates the agreed order of repayment, where the borrower has given a contractual undertaking to the lender of the senior debt, with a corresponding acknowledgement by the lender of the subordinated debt, in a multiparity agreement known as a Subordination Agreement or Deed of Priority.

JUNK BONDS

A device used extensively in the USA during the 1980s whereby high-yielding, unsecured debt is used to finance MERGERS AND ACQUISITIONS and other corporate activity. The debt is recorded in a PROMISSORY NOTE or BOND issued to investors. Invariably the bond is unsecured and is subordinated to other debt of the company. This combination makes the investment risky, hence the name junk. At the peak of the 1980s takeover activity investors queued to buy junk bonds, attracted by their high yields. For many it was tears before bedtime. Some bonds became completely worthless as the issuing companies stalled on the interest payments, and investors began to understand the true implications of a junk bond. In the search for culprits a few witches were paraded through the streets, given public duckings on the ducking chair or burned at the stake. This made the investors feel a little better, but they did not get any money back.

JURAT

The prescribed form of words at the end of an AFFIDAVIT which show when and where it was sworn.

JURISPRUDENCE
The philosophy of law; the study of law and legal systems.

> *Is the law sin? God forbid. Nay, I had not known sin, but by the law.*
> The Bible, Romans, 7:7

JURY
A group of 12 (or 9 for an INQUEST or 24 for a GRAND JURY) upstanding members of the community selected at random to participate in the judicial process by deciding issues of fact in the competing arguments presented to the court by the combatants. In theory the JUDGE determines issues of law and directs the jury on how to interpret the evidence against the background of the law, leaving the jury to decide on issues of fact. In criminal trials this usually requires the jury to decide whether or not the DEFENDANT did what the prosecution alleges and what was his state of mind at the time; for example, did he mean to do it? The use of a jury in civil actions in the UK is now rare (except in DEFAMATION cases), and the judge is required to decide on both legal and factual issues. There is a move to eliminate the jury from complex fraud and other criminal trials, supposedly on the ground that the general public is not quite up to understanding the intricacies of financial dealings. Potential jurors may applaud this patronising arrogance; not many people relish the thought of spending up to six months listening to the interminable drone of legal arguments about financial misdeeds.

> *A jury consists of twelve persons chosen to decide who has the better lawyer.*
> Robert Frost

JUSTICE OF THE PEACE
A MAGISTRATE.

K

KITE MARK
A logo, which resembles the shape of a traditional kite, put on UK goods to signify that they meet official safety standards.

KNOCK-FOR-KNOCK
There is an accident involving two cars. Both are damaged. Both owners notify their respective insurers. Rather than argue over who is to blame, the insurers agree between themselves to bear the cost of repairs for their own insured drivers. For the insurers, this knock-for-knock approach is an efficient way of disposing of a claim with minimum effort. For the innocent driver that did not cause the accident, it is an unfair record of an insurance claim against his name.

KNOW-HOW
An example of where the law tries to be adaptable to the changing needs of commercial life. Know-how was understood as a commercial term before getting legal recognition. It is the skill and knowledge required to effect a commercial or industrial or business function. As far as it relates to property rights, it can be seen as trade secrets or confidential information and its legal protection lies in the law of COPYRIGHT or PATENT. It frequently appears in commercial contracts (see TECHNOLOGY TRANSFER) where one party agrees to provide know-how to the other in return for payment and promises of confidentiality.

LABOR LAW
The US equivalent to UK employment law, being the network of laws that governs relations between employers and employees.

LABOR UNION
The US equivalent to a UK trades union, being an organisation of workers to represent their interests collectively and in dealings with their employers.

LACHES
A principle of EQUITY that restricts someone's right to complain of a wrong if he or she has delayed or neglected to complain when first becoming aware of it.

A litigant is a person about to give up his skin for the hope of retaining his bones.
Ambrose Bierce, 1887

LADING (BILL OF)
A formal receipt issued by a shipper to confirm that specified goods have been loaded on the ship. A bill of lading is often one of the documents the seller of goods must present to the bank in order to claim payment of the sale price under a LETTER OF CREDIT.

LADY DAY
March 25th, a QUARTER DAY.

LAND CERTIFICATE
An official document, issued by the LAND REGISTRY, that records who is the owner of specified land in the UK. It contains information about the land, such as its official description and details of previous owners (since first registration), and refers to other documents that contain rights affecting the land. If there are any outstanding charges or other SECURITY interests attaching to the land these will also be recorded on the certificate, which is then known as a CHARGE CERTIFICATE.

LANDING CHARGES

A general term to cover customs duties and other charges imposed on goods being imported into a country.

LANDING ORDER

An official permit issued to allow goods to be imported and stored in a BONDED WAREHOUSE without the payment of customs duties.

LANDMARK

A landmark decision is a judgement delivered by a court which creates an important legal principle as a precedent for the future. See the application of precedent at COMMON LAW.

LAND REGISTRY

A UK government office that runs the system of land registration and issues land certificates (or charge certificates, as the case may be) to landowners. Largely based on the Law of Property Act 1925, one of the most enduring and successful examples of modern LEGISLATION, land registration has created some order in UK land law where previously there was chaos. Registration is guaranteed TITLE, so as a prospective purchaser of land you can inspect the register to confirm that your prospective vendor is indeed the owner. When the sale and purchase are completed, you can apply to the Land Registry for your name to be registered as the owner. The registry will then re-issue the Land Certificate to you. Most of England and Wales are now covered by this land registration system, although there are pockets of unregistered land awaiting registration at their next transfer.

LAPSED LEGACY

A gift under a WILL that cannot take effect because the person to whom it is directed died before the person who made the will.

LARCENY

An old-fashioned word for theft, now obsolete in

the UK but still in use in the USA and elsewhere.

Morality cannot be legislated, but behaviour can be regulated. Judicial decrees may not change the heart, but they can restrain the heartless.
Martin Luther King, 1963

LAST IN, FIRST OUT
A policy based on an arbitrary rule for selecting employees for REDUNDANCY. If an employer is forced to make redundancies, it selects those employees who joined latest to be first for the chop. It is also a method (popular in the USA) used in accountancy to calculate the cost of stocks where it is difficult to determine which specific items remain and which have been used.

LATENT DEFECT
A fault that remains hidden for some time but eventually appears and becomes an issue in a dispute between the person who suffers from the defect and the person who is alleged to have caused it. For example, the foundations of a building may have been negligently constructed by the original builder, but no damage is apparent until many years later. The legal issue is the LIMITATION PERIOD for such latent defects: should time run from the original negligent act or from the date the defect is discovered? Under current English law, the answer is the date on which a reasonable person should have been aware that there was a problem. It is a fudge that probably causes more uncertainty than it solves.

LAW CENTRE
An office staffed by lawyers, usually funded by a governmental or local authority, who offer legal advice to the public free of charge. Not highly paid, these lawyers tackle a mountain of social and domestic issues (often outside the bounds of legal practice) and deserve far more praise than they ever get.

Law Commission

A permanent body of respected jurists that reviews English law on a continuing basis and recommends changes to it. The recommendations are either adopted or ignored by the government of the day. If adopted, they find their way through PARLIAMENT and emerge as new law in the form of LEGISLATION.

Law list

An annual list of barristers and solicitors licensed to practise in England and Wales.

Law lords

The name given to the UK's most senior judges, including the LORD CHANCELLOR, who sit in the House of Lords (the upper house of the UK PARLIAMENT) and provide the membership of the Judicial Committee of the House of Lords, which is the highest court of APPEAL in the UK.

The lawyer's truth is not Truth, but consistency or a consistent expediency.
Henry David Thoreau, 1849

Law officers

The Law Officers of the Crown are the ATTORNEY-GENERAL and the SOLICITOR-GENERAL in England and Wales, and the LORD ADVOCATE and the solicitor-general in SCOTLAND.

Law reports

Publications of decisions, including the judges' reasoning, delivered as judgements at the end of a trial. The law reports provide a guide to precedent as set out in CASE LAW and are the tangible embodiment of the COMMON LAW. The various publications of law reports are known by their initials, such as the WLR (Weekly Law Reports) and AELR (All England Law Reports).

Law school

In the UK a law school is a postgraduate college

that prepares students for solicitors' or barristers' qualifying examinations. It is still possible to enter a law school without a degree (for example, as a LEGAL EXECUTIVE seeking to re-qualify), but now the majority are graduates. In the USA it is usually a law faculty at a university where students, invariably postgraduates, take a law degree as a second degree. Thereafter they take the BAR EXAMINATION to qualify as a lawyer in the state of their choice.

LAW SOCIETY
The professional body of solicitors. It appoints them, monitors complaints against them, regulates their professional conduct and strikes them off the register when they are found guilty of serious misconduct. It also represents solicitors in discussions with the government on new laws and their administration.

LEADER
In a complex English court case each side will have two barristers: a leader and a JUNIOR. The leader, usually but not necessarily a QUEEN'S COUNSEL, is the main BARRISTER who conducts the case and dictates the strategy. The junior plays a supporting role and does all the hard work.

LEADING QUESTION
If you are an advocate, asking questions of a witness in court (either in EXAMINATION IN CHIEF or CROSS EXAMINATION), the rules of evidence require you to present your questions in an open, objective manner to allow the witness to answer fairly. You should not ask a question in a way that suggests a particular answer: this is a leading question. In practice, of course, advocates use leading questions all the time; if they did not the pace of the trial would slow almost to a standstill. The JUDGE should step in, however, when the advocate appears to be leading the witness towards giving answers that may not represent his or her true evidence.

L

LEASE

A written agreement between a landlord and a tenant whereby the landlord allows the tenant to have possession of land or buildings (or part of a building), or equipment (as in a FINANCE LEASE), in return for the payment of rent. A lease can have a fixed duration or can run indefinitely subject to a right of termination on either side. In all jurisdictions leases of land or buildings (REAL ESTATE) are regulated by LEGISLATION that supplements the parties' rights and duties.

> *In law, what plea so tainted and corrupt, but, being seasoned with a gracious voice, obscures the show of evil.*
> William Shakespeare, *The Merchant of Venice*

LEASE BACK

See SALE AND LEASE BACK.

LEASEHOLD ENFRANCHISEMENT

The right of a leaseholder to buy the FREEHOLD of a property he or she holds on a LEASE.

LEGAL AID

A scheme established and financed by the UK government under which a person with limited financial resources can get free or subsidised legal advice. You apply to the Legal Aid Board with details of your case and your personal means. If accepted by the board, the Legal Aid Fund will pay all your SOLICITOR's fees, BARRISTER's fees and other legal costs (but you may have to make a contribution to the fund). Critics of the scheme point out that most people have to be extremely poor before they qualify and, more seriously, that there are some theoretically poor but clearly rich people who get legal aid. In any event, it does not help the broad range of middle income-earners who cannot afford to pursue a legal case but whose income disqualifies them from legal aid.

LEGACY

A gift of money or personal effects (but not land, which is a DEVISE) under a WILL.

LEGAL EXECUTIVE

A clerk in a SOLICITOR's office who has passed the qualifying examinations of the Institute of Legal Executives but who has not qualified as a solicitor. A legal executive should not be confused with a PARALEGAL. Many legal executives have extensive experience (which can cover any aspect of law), practise largely without supervision and can be a valuable (and lucrative) asset to a solicitor's practice.

LEGAL MEMORY

See TIME IMMEMORIAL.

LEGAL OPINION

Traditionally, a legal opinion is a formal, written and carefully reasoned statement of the law given by a respected lawyer (often a BARRISTER). More recently, it is a formal letter of advice, in common use in the USA and gaining acceptance elsewhere, issued by a law firm to one of the parties at the CLOSING of a CONTRACT (usually a MERGERS AND ACQUISITIONS transaction, a financing arrangement or similar corporate transaction). The letter confirms that the other contracting party (usually the law firm's client) has taken the necessary corporate steps to execute the contract and that the contract will be valid, binding and enforceable in accordance with its terms. This process, of course, is a means of getting another party (the law firm) on the hook if things go awry and the contracting party seeks to wriggle out of its obligations. The form of a legal opinion has become largely standardised by convention and, unsurprisingly, is given careful review by the law firm before it is issued.

LEGISLATION

Laws enacted by PARLIAMENT in the form of statutes or acts of Parliament. (Contrast with CASE LAW.)

LEMON

In the vernacular of the MERGERS AND ACQUISITIONS lawyer, a lemon is a bad deal, a bad investment or a transaction destined for failure. In US jargon, as explained by a fictional corporate raider, Gordon Gekko, in the film "Wall Street", a bad deal is "a dog" and a very bad deal "a dog with fleas". A lemon is compared with a PLUM. There are more lemons than plums.

Certain laws have not been written, but they are more fixed than all the written laws.
Seneca the Elder, 100 AD

LET-OUT CLAUSE

A colloquialism referring to a clause in a CONTRACT that allows a party to avoid performing its obligations when certain events occur.

LETTER BEFORE ACTION

This is your last chance or else. A letter before action is sent by a lawyer on behalf of a client giving the addressee a last chance (usually within a stated time) to comply with the client's demands or face LITIGATION.

LETTER OF ALLOTMENT

A formal notice issued by a company which tells applicants for shares how many they have been allotted.

LETTER OF CREDIT

If nobody trusts anybody in business, absolutely nobody trusts anybody when they are doing business with somebody in another country. To overcome some of this prejudice, the international banking community invented a procedure to guarantee payment for export sales. For example, a seller in Sheffield agrees to sell machine parts to a buyer in Baghdad. The contract requires the buyer to arrange a letter of credit to guarantee payment. The buyer asks its bank in Baghdad to issue the letter of credit, which it sends to its correspondent bank in the UK, preferably near Sheffield. The letter of credit records a list of documents that the seller must deliver to the bank in Sheffield in order to claim payment. This list comprises the evidence to show that the correct goods have been delivered to Baghdad in conformance with the contract. The documents may include a certificate of origin to show where the goods were made, a bill of LADING to prove they were shipped, proof of payment of customs duties, an acknowledgement of delivery and so on. If the seller is able to present all the specified documents to the Sheffield bank, the bank must pay the sum specified in the letter of credit. This is the seller's guarantee of payment.

Let all the laws be clear, uniform, and precise; to interpret laws is almost always to corrupt them.
Voltaire, 1764

LETTER OF INTENT

A document recording someone's intention to do something, often setting out the basic terms of a business transaction, which will subsequently be confirmed in a formal CONTRACT. The big issue is whether or not the letter of intent is binding on the person who gives it. Usually it is not meant to be binding and should be littered with qualifying expressions like SUBJECT TO CONTRACT. Without these qualifications you can find yourself bound to something you may not have intended. In this case a letter of intent has become a contract.

LETTING

A LEASE or the property governed by a lease.

LEVERAGED BUY-OUT

A MANAGEMENT BUY-OUT financed by a high level of borrowing (leverage) secured on the assets acquired. The term leverage is more readily understood in the USA than in Europe. In the UK the rules in the COMPANIES ACTS against FINANCIAL ASSISTANCE (the restrictions on a company in providing financial assistance for the acquisition of its own shares) restrict the scope for leverage in a corporate takeover. If an acquirer buys shares in a TARGET COMPANY it cannot use the target's assets as SECURITY on borrowings to provide the acquisition finance. These rules do not apply to assets deals, where the acquirer purchases the UNDERTAKING or assets of the target rather than its shares and accordingly the prospects for leverage are higher.

LEX

Latin for "law", as in *lex fori* (the law of the place where the case is being heard), *lex loci* (the law of the place where the act was done) and so on.

LIABILITY

Your comeuppance; that which you must do or pay. Liability is the foundation of the law and most of its rules, whether in CONTRACT or TORT, are devised to work out who is liable to whom for the loss or damage caused by the particular circumstances. The rules of law, rather like the rules of war, must find a winner and a loser. A draw, for the most part, is not acceptable. The winner gets compensation; the loser gets liability. This underlines the law's tendency towards moral judgements, as opposed to economic or political judgements. Liability concentrates on fault. It is your fault so you are liable, regardless of whether you are best placed or able to bear the loss.

LIBEL

See DEFAMATION.

> *Somehow, our sense of justice never turns in its sleep till long after the sense of injustice in others has been thoroughly aroused.*
> Max Beerbohm, 1920

LIBOR

An acronym for the London inter-bank offered rate, the rate of interest at which banks in London lend money to each other. The rate is set at 11am in London every working day. LIBOR is often used in financing agreements to set the interest rate for a transaction by reference to the market rate. Thus a lender might agree to advance a loan to a borrower at, say, 2% above LIBOR. In banking jargon the fractions of the percentages above LIBOR are known as points. If you borrow at 2% above LIBOR you are borrowing at 200 points, 1.75% above means 175 points and so on. This jargon serves its purpose of adding a mystique to the world of high finance and neatly confuses the uninitiated (usually, of course, the borrower).

LICENCE
A licence allows a person to enjoy rights owned by another. It can suggest enjoyment at the gift of the owner, such as a licence to occupy land terminable at will, or it can be a fully enforceable right, such as a licence to use a TRADE MARK on full commercial terms including royalties. A licence, which allows someone to use rights owned by another, is distinguishable from an ASSIGNMENT, which is the transfer of ownership of those rights.

LIEN
This is a right to retain possession (but not ownership) of goods until you have been paid for services rendered in respect of them. For example, if you take your car to a garage for repairs, the garage is entitled to keep it (by claiming a lien on it) until you pay the repair costs. A lien is an ENCUMBRANCE.

LIFE INTEREST
An ownership right that is valid only during someone's lifetime. If your rich aunt gives you a life interest in the family mansion, with the REMAINDER passing to your children after your death, you are entitled to occupy and enjoy it but you are not allowed to dispose of it or pass it on to anyone but your children, who will automatically become entitled to it on your death.

LIMITATION PERIOD

The statute of limitations is a rule, found in every modern jurisdiction, which allows a limited period of time (in the UK, usually six years) for someone to start court proceedings to enforce a right or claim compensation for a wrong. The limitation period usually starts from the date the right was impeded or the wrong committed, but there are exceptions to this (see LATENT DEFECT). Another exception applies in the case of a breach of a CONTRACT executed under SEAL (that is a DEED), where the law allows 12 years for someone to bring an action.

LINCOLN'S INN

One of the four INNS OF COURT.

LIQUIDATION

The closing or WINDING UP of a company and the sale of all its assets for the benefit of any creditors and, thereafter, if there is a surplus of assets over liabilities, for its MEMBERS. The procedure for the liquidation of a UK company is described in detail in the COMPANIES ACTS. A liquidation can be ordered by the court, usually on the application of a creditor (a compulsory liquidation), or it can be implemented by the company's own members (a voluntary liquidation). Either way, it is the end of the game for the company.

LISTED COMPANY

A company whose shares are listed on a stock exchange. By definition a listed company cannot be a PRIVATE COMPANY, since its shares are offered to the public, initially by means of a FLOTATION. A listed company must be a PUBLIC COMPANY, but not every public company is a listed company. To maintain its listing, a UK listed company must abide by the rules (known as the listing rules) of the stock exchange, which are published in a handy yellow book known as the yellow book.

LITIGATION

This is the real thing. The trial. The court case. In

the final analysis all law has to be tested and tried in a courtroom. Litigation is the act of pursuing a claim or defending a right through the courts. It produces a winner and a loser (unlike, say, MEDIATION, which usually tries to find some acceptable compromise between the two sides). The only certainty in litigation is that it will be expensive, usually for both parties. In the USA it is rare for either party to recover its legal costs from the other. In the UK a court will order the loser to pay the winner's costs, but frequently this award covers only part of the winner's expenses. The only people that really enjoy litigation are litigation lawyers (trial lawyers in the USA), who make a bundle out of it.

For certain people, after fifty, litigation takes the place of sex.
Gore Vidal

LOCKOUT
An industrial dispute in which an employer closes the factory or workplace to prevent the workers from working.

LOCK-OUT AGREEMENT
Also known as a shut-out agreement. This is a CONTRACT between a potential buyer and an intending seller (usually of a company, but it can be any asset) whereby the seller agrees not to engage in negotiations with another potential buyer for a stated period of time. This is to enable the identified prospective buyer to carry out DUE DILIGENCE or to arrange finance or otherwise to get itself organised to sign the main contract for the acquisition of the asset. In recent times there has been some CASE LAW in the UK on whether a lockout agreement is unenforceable on the grounds that it is an agreement to agree or an agreement not to agree, but it is a useful commercial tool and the courts seem to have accepted its legality on the strained argument that it is an agreement not to negotiate.

L

Locus standi

Latin for "a place to stand". It refers to the right to appear before a court. In England and Wales a BARRISTER has *locus standi* in the Court of APPEAL but a SOLICITOR does not.

Lord Advocate

A member of the UK government as one of the LAW OFFICERS, the Lord Advocate is head of the judiciary in SCOTLAND.

Lord Chancellor

A member of the UK government who presides over debates in the House of Lords (the upper house of the UK PARLIAMENT) and is responsible for the administration of the judicial system. Judges are formally appointed by the sovereign on the recommendation of the government of the day. The Lord Chancellor's department is responsible for making these recommendations and, effectively, appoints judges.

Lord Justice

The title given to a JUDGE who sits in the Court of APPEAL, the intermediate appeal court in the UK legal system. The title is abbreviated to LJ written after the judge's name, as in Denning LJ.

Justice is always violent to the party offending, for every man is innocent in his own eyes.
Daniel Defoe, 1702

Lord of Appeal

A member of the House of Lords who, as a senior JUDGE, sits when the House is acting as the final court of appeal (see SEPARATION OF POWERS).

M&A
See MERGERS AND ACQUISITIONS.

MAGISTRATE
A JUSTICE OF THE PEACE, an official (usually part-time, unpaid and without any legal qualification) who presides in a lower court (a magistrate's court) to judge minor offences and some family cases. A stipendiary magistrate, who carries out the same duties, usually full-time, is legally qualified and salaried.

MALA IN SE
Latin for "wrongs in themselves". Some acts are so bad that they are crimes by their very nature, such as murder. Other acts, such as jaywalking, are not crimes in themselves but are made into crimes by law. These are called *mala prohibita*, which means "forbidden wrongs".

MALFEASANCE
An unlawful act; as opposed to MISFEASANCE, which is carrying out an act improperly. Malpractice is reserved for professional malfeasors or misfeasors, such as lawyers or doctors acting improperly, unlawfully or unprofessionally and thereby leaving themselves open to LIABILITY to anyone who may have suffered as a result.

MANAGEMENT BUY-IN
Similar to a MANAGEMENT BUY-OUT (MBO), except that instead of the target company being acquired by its own managers, it is acquired by a management team from outside the company. The transaction follows the same format as an MBO, with the management team backed by finance from a bank or venture capitalist. A management buy-in (MBI) is often a subsequent strategic move to an MBO. The management team acquires its own company as a first step, then pulls off an MBI of a competitor to expand its trading base.

MANAGEMENT BUY-OUT
A management buy-out (MBO) is the acquisition of

a company by its own managers. In a typical example, the managers ally themselves with a VENTURE CAPITAL provider (who supplies the money and calls the shots) to form a new company (imaginatively called Newco), which buys the shares (or the assets) of the managers' employing company (inevitably called Oldco). Besides the acquisition contracts between Newco and the owners (shareholders) of Oldco, there are extensive agreements between the venture capitalist and the management team. The venture capitalist will expect an opportunity to liquidate its investment within the medium term, often five years, so it will set financial targets for Newco which act as incentives (through increased ownership participation) for the management team to achieve this. The so-called exit of the venture capitalist is as delicate as the original MBO acquisition, particularly as there are only a few options.

- FLOTATION on a stockmarket, allowing the venture capitalist (and the management team) to sell shares in Newco to the public.
- A trade sale, where Newco's shares are sold to a single acquirer, usually a larger company in the same business sector, which invariably requires a majority interest and frequently wants 100% control. This is ironic since the management team's original aim was to free itself from the ownership of Oldco and they now find themselves back in the arms of a devil they did not know.
- The replacement of the venture capitalist by another venture capitalist, if the managers can persuade another banker to back Newco for a few more years.

There are many successful MBO transactions, notably where Newco is able to take advantage of good economic conditions to get a flotation on the stockmarket, and many managers have used this mechanism to make a fortune. However, some seeds fall on stony ground and the managers (with their venture capital backers) may struggle to make it work. (For variations on the MBO theme, see MANAGEMENT BUY-IN and BIMBO.)

MANDAMUS
Latin for "we command". It is an order or instruction from a higher court to a lower court. For example, a citizen may apply to a higher court for a WRIT of mandamus to require a lower court to rehear a case on the ground that the original hearing was flawed by a procedural irregularity.

> *There are not enough jails, not enough*
> *policemen, not enough courts to enforce a law*
> *not supported by the people.*
> Hubert H. Humphrey, 1965

MANUAL
In the USA it is the official guide to the procedures of the houses of CONGRESS. In the rest of the world it is the instructions on how to use your washing machine.

MAREVA INJUNCTION
This important weapon in English LITIGATION is named after the first case in which this type of INJUNCTION was granted (*Mareva Compania Naviera SA v International Bulk Carriers SA*). It allows a PLAINTIFF to ask the court to grant an injunction to prevent the DEFENDANT from moving assets outside the jurisdiction of the court so that they remain within the court's control (and therefore within the plaintiff's grasp) if and when judgement is granted in favour of the plaintiff. There have to be good reasons to suspect that the assets are likely to be moved; for example, a foreign-owned ship is about to depart from a UK port or a foreign company is about to withdraw its assets. The application is usually heard EX PARTE.

MARKETABLE
Something that is readily saleable. Marketable TITLE is title to property that allows such property to be sold because it is free of ENCUMBRANCE.

MARKET CAPITALISATION
A rough and ready valuation of a PUBLIC COMPANY taken by multiplying the current price (the price at which they are currently changing hands on the stock exchange) of its shares by the number of shares in issue at the time. This is known as market cap to the MERGERS AND ACQUISITIONS fraternity.

MARKET PRICE
The estimated price at which something is expected to be sold in an arm's-length transaction between a willing seller and a willing buyer. This formula can, of course, produce a variable range of results unless a particular market publishes its prices continuously, as does a stock exchange.

The jury, passing on the prisoner's life, may in the sworn twelve have a thief or two guiltier than him they try.
William Shakespeare, *Measure for Measure*

MASTER
A type of JUDGE. A master is an official of either the QUEEN'S BENCH DIVISION or the CHANCERY DIVISION of the HIGH COURT, who hears and deals with preliminary issues in a case on its way to trial. The PRACTICE MASTER is available to litigants without an appointment (turn up, line up) and will give general directions on the conduct of proceedings. The practice master (whoever it may be) is notoriously overworked, overstressed and short-tempered with badly prepared solicitors. A TAXING MASTER is appointed to assess the costs of a case, where one party (the loser) is ordered to pay the costs of the other (the winner).

MASTER OF THE ROLLS
A senior JUDGE who presides over the Civil Division (as opposed to the Criminal Division) of the English Court of APPEAL. The Master of the Rolls is also responsible for admitting solicitors to the Roll of Solicitors (confirming their qualification to act) and every year has to sign thousands of admissions certificates.

M

MATRIMONIAL CAUSES
Court proceedings relating to marriage or, more usually, divorce and the rights of one spouse against the other.

MBI
See MANAGEMENT BUY-IN.

MBO
See MANAGEMENT BUY-OUT.

MECHANICAL REPRODUCTION RIGHTS
Part of the law of COPYRIGHT. The right (usually granted by the copyright holder under a LICENCE in return for a ROYALTY) for someone to make and exploit a recording of some music or a photographic copy of written or graphic material.

MEDIATION
A trendy marketing technique is to use an old idea that is repackaged with a new image and sold as a new idea. Mediation predates LITIGATION by a couple of million years, so we can presume that two warring cavemen would sometimes use the services of a third caveman to act as intermediary – a mediator – to help them solve their quarrel. However, within the last few years it has been repackaged, first in the USA, then in Europe and around the world, as alternative dispute resolution, with its compulsory three-letter acronym, ADR. The word alternative is supposed to emphasise another route besides litigation, which with its attendant costs and all-or-nothing verdict strikes fear into the hearts of businessmen everywhere. Other than that there is very little new about it.

One innovation is that mediation has become more formalised, although undefined flexibility is still its strong point, and some rules of the game have been put on paper by organisations that offer their services as mediation agencies. Mostly the mediator strives to find a compromise acceptable to both sides; unlike in litigation, it is rare to find an outright winner. The carrot is a reasonably quick and cheap means to settle a commercial dispute in a reasonably amicable atmosphere, which may even allow continued trading relations between the parties. The stick is failure to settle, which almost inevitably means litigation. (See also ARBITRATION.)

> *A man's respect for law and order exists in precise relationship to the size of his paycheck.*
> Adam Clayton Powell, 1967

MEMBERS
The members of a company are its shareholders. A meeting of the members is a GENERAL MEETING.

MEMORANDUM OF ASSOCIATION
In contrast to the ARTICLES OF ASSOCIATION, which deal with internal affairs, a company's memorandum of association records the OBJECTS and POWERS of the company in its dealings with outsiders. The objects are the purposes for which the company was founded. If a company purports to do something that is not within the scope of its objects, the act is ULTRA VIRES and can be void. However, the harshness of this rule has been softened by legislation imported into the UK through EU legislation. If a person deals with a company in good faith and has no knowledge of any restriction or omission in its objects, he is entitled to assume there is none and his dealings will be upheld.

MEMORANDUM OF SATISFACTION
A document, filed at COMPANIES HOUSE in the UK, which shows that a company has satisfied (that is, repaid and secured the release of) a MORTGAGE or CHARGE.

MENS REA
Latin for "guilty mind". To be convicted of some crimes, the prosecution has to prove that you intended to carry out the alleged offence and accordingly that you had a guilty mind. *Mens rea* provides the distinction between murder and manslaughter: did you mean to kill?

MERCHANTABLE QUALITY

This is an IMPLIED TERM in many contracts for the sale of goods. In the UK it is implied by the SALE OF GOODS ACTS, and, to make it more understandable to non-lawyers, it has been replaced by the colourless term SATISFACTORY QUALITY. Notwithstanding that it can be excluded by agreement between the parties, the term implies a WARRANTY by the seller that the goods will be of a quality that is commonly expected for goods of that type and that they correspond to any sample or description given by the seller in advertising material.

Anyone who takes it upon himself, on his private authority, to break a bad law, thereby authorises everyone else to break the good ones.
Denis Diderot, 1796

MERGERS AND ACQUISITIONS

Mergers between companies and the acquisition of one company by another; also the name given to the department of an investment bank charged with handling them. Mergers and acquisitions (M&A) activity is more prevalent in economies with strong, egalitarian stockmarkets, such as the UK and the USA, than it is in Japan or continental Europe.

The claim to be a mergers and acquisitions lawyer was in the 1980s a necessary badge of the gung-ho, yuppie lawyer seeking a piece of the action in the epidemic of corporate takeovers at the end of the decade. It meant all-night negotiating sessions, deal-breaking hurdles to be overcome and lots of money in fees. The name, and the attendant reputation, faded with the decrease in takeover activity as the worldwide recession arrived in the early 1990s, but it has made a come-back in the mid-1990s as corporate activity has resumed.

MESNE PROFITS

Along the lines of QUANTUM MERUIT, an action for mesne profits is a claim by a landowner for money he thinks he ought to be paid in place of

rent by a person who is in unlawful occupation of
his land.

MESSUAGE
A house where untidy people live? Messuage is an
archaic English word derived from French law referring to the land and buildings that comprise a
domestic dwelling.

MEZZANINE FINANCE
An intermediate (and expensive) form of finance
or JUNIOR DEBT, often used in VENTURE CAPITAL transactions, which sits comfortably between a company's EQUITY CAPITAL and its SENIOR DEBT.
Mezzanine finance is usually unsecured and subordinated to (ranking after) the secured loans, but
in a WINDING UP it would rank ahead of the equity
capital. This means mezzanine finance is comparatively risky and proportionately expensive; typically, its interest rate will be one or two
percentage points higher than the senior debt.
Notwithstanding its SUBORDINATION, the high cost
of maintaining the mezzanine finance will encourage the holders of the senior debt to consent to its
early repayment and thereby relieve some pressure on the company's finance costs.

> *If I were in your place, I'd go over and give
> Brown a drink and settle this dispute in ten
> minutes. But, as your lawyer, I advise you to sue
> him. Let no arrogant, domineering pirate like
> Brown trample on your sacred rights. Assert your
> manhood and your courage. And I need the
> money.*
> Joseph Hodges Choate, 1890

MICHAELMAS
One of the four sittings (or terms) in the annual
calendar of the courts in England and Wales.
Michaelmas Day is September 29th, a QUARTER DAY.

MIDDLE TEMPLE
One of the four INNS OF COURT.

MIDSUMMER DAY
June 24th, a QUARTER DAY.

MINOR
A person who does not have full legal capacity because he or she is too young. In the UK and the USA a minor is someone aged under 18 (see NEXT FRIEND).

MINUTES
The minutes of a meeting are the written record of what was said and decided at the meeting. Typically, the first item on an agenda of a regular meeting is the consideration of the minutes of the previous meeting. If it is agreed that the minutes fairly record the business discussed, the chairman is instructed to sign them and they become the formal record of the meeting. In LITIGATION the minutes of order are prepared by one party and presented to the court as a draft, for issue as a formal order, if the JUDGE agrees that they accurately reflect what he meant to say.

MISDIRECTION
In COMMON LAW jurisdictions, such as the UK and the USA, an APPEAL can be made against a decision of a court only if it is based on an issue of law, not a finding of fact. If a JURY decides that the DEFENDANT was at the scene of the crime at the relevant time, he cannot appeal solely on the ground that the evidence suggested he was not. However, if in his SUMMING UP the JUDGE has given the jury wrong directions on a point of law, such as how they should interpret the evidence relating to the defendant's presence or absence, this is an issue of law and is open to appeal. Misdirection of a jury is a common ground of appeal in criminal cases.

MISFEASANCE
See MALFEASANCE.

MISJOINDER
Wrongly joining someone as a party to a LITIGATION action.

MISREPRESENTATION

If you induce someone to enter into a CONTRACT by falsely stating information that is material to the contract, the person may be able to deny the contract by reason of your misrepresentation. This will depend on the seriousness of the misrepresentation and whether it was innocent (that is, you were not aware that the information was false) or fraudulent (that is, you were fully aware and indeed intended to deceive them). The misrepresentation may also amount to a TORT, giving the other party a right of action against you for DAMAGES arising as a result of the misrepresentation. This area of English law is one of the few exceptions to the principle of freedom of contract. Borrowing the idea of GOOD FAITH more commonly found in the continental systems of CIVIL LAW, these rules require contracting parties to play fairly, up to a point.

If a lawyer's hand is freed, sir, he steals your whole estate.
William Makepeace Thackeray, 1861

MISTAKE

As with MISREPRESENTATION, mistake is another rare exception to the principle of freedom of CONTRACT. This basic principle of COMMON LAW says that contracting parties should be free to make whatever agreement they may choose, even if it is plainly a bad deal for one of them, and the law will not interfere. In contrast, CIVIL LAW systems frequently impose a duty of GOOD FAITH, which requires both parties to act fairly. The doctrine of mistake is an exception that can be applied to dismantle a contract – that is, to prevent one party enforcing it against the other – where the second party can show that a genuine mistake existed in the minds of the parties at the time the contract was made. The mistake has to be sufficiently serious and must be fundamental to the contract; for example, one party thought it was buying mung beans and the other thought it was selling wong beans.

M

Using an example such as this, legal purists can argue that mistake is not truly an exception to the principle of freedom of contract. In fact there was no contract at all since the parties were never "in one mind" as to the terms of the contract and so the contract was not validly formed in the first place.

MITIGATION
If you have suffered loss or DAMAGES as a result of a TORT or a breach of CONTRACT caused by some-one else, you are entitled to claim against them for the amount of the loss or damages (which is their LIABILITY to you). However, you cannot just sit back and let the loss get worse (thinking that you can claim it all from the other party); you have a duty to take reasonable steps to prevent the loss from mounting up. This is the duty to mitigate your loss. Mitigation also refers to the list of ex-cuses your counsel puts forward on your behalf when you have been convicted of a crime and the JUDGE is considering your punishment.

MMC
See MONOPOLIES AND MERGERS COMMISSION.

M'NAGHTEN RULES
A good example of sound legal reasoning that has stood the test of time, although in this case it is in-sane legal reasoning. In 1843 the House of Lords considered the case of *R. v M'Naghten* and there-upon laid down a set of rules for judges to deter-mine whether a person charged with a crime is insane to the extent that he or she should not be found guilty of the alleged crime. To prove insan-ity, it has to be established that the person did not know what he was doing, or did not know that his action was wrong, because of a diseased mind. These basic rules, with some refinement, have been in use for 150 years.

MONOPOLIES AND MERGERS COMMISSION
The UK regulatory body that is given the task of reviewing proposed MERGERS AND ACQUISITIONS of

UK companies to ensure that the ensuing combination does not create a monopoly or any other undesirable, anti-competitive market position. The Monopolies and Mergers Commission (MMC) reports to the secretary of state for trade and industry (a government minister), who has power to prevent a proposed merger from going ahead if he believes it might adversely affect the public interest. The MMC also reviews restrictive trade practices, such as alleged cartels, to impose ANTI-TRUST legislation and maintain a free market within permitted boundaries.

MOOT
To debate competing arguments in an attempt to establish an agreed or decided principle. A moot court, often arranged for law students to practise their advocacy skills, will pick a knotty legal issue and ask two teams to take the roles of representing the PLAINTIFF and DEFENDANT respectively. Someone takes the role of the JUDGE, who hears the arguments, tests them in debate and pronounces a judgement based on the merits of the presentations.

> *The law is a sort of hocus-pocus science, that*
> *smiles in your face while it picks your pocket.*
> Charles Dickens, *Oliver Twist*

MORTGAGE
A form of SECURITY given as a guarantee that a debtor will pay his debt. The debtor (the mortgagor) signs a DEED which gives the creditor or lender (the mortgagee) an interest in the mortgaged property and authorises the mortgagee to take possession of and sell the property if the mortgagor fails to pay the debt on the agreed terms. A legal mortgage is where the mortgagee acquires a full legal interest in the mortgaged property (in the case of REAL ESTATE, by registering its interest on the ownership register). An equitable mortgage is less formal (where the mortgagee does not register its interest, but takes

possession of the TITLE deeds to prevent the mortgagor selling the property without its consent).

MUNIMENTS
Another archaic term of English law, muniments are the deeds of TITLE for a parcel of REAL ESTATE.

MURPHY'S LAW
Not yet acknowledged by the more sophisticated systems of JURISPRUDENCE, but accepted as a fact by most right-minded people, this principle states that if there is any possibility that something will go wrong, it invariably does.

MUTATIS MUTANDIS
Latin for "change and change about". The same rules or principles will apply in a similar situation with different, but analogous, facts.

MUTUAL COMPANY
An insurance company or similar organisation that is owned by its policyholders rather than any shareholders.

NAPOLEONIC CODE
The codification of the CIVIL LAW, first ordered by Napoleon for the laws of France in the early 19th century.

NATURALISATION
The grant of citizenship to a foreigner. To apply for naturalisation in the UK, you have to live there continuously for at least five years and show that you have become established in the British way of life.

NATURAL LAW
A theory of JURISPRUDENCE that there are general principles of law, akin to morals, which all societies and civilisations recognise as fundamental to justice and good order. For example, it is a principle of natural law that a court should not pronounce judgement on a case without hearing arguments for both sides.

NATURAL PERSON
A legal person can be an individual, a PARTNERSHIP, a validly established company, a sovereign state or a government body. Of these, only an individual is a natural person; the others are artificial.

NEGLIGENCE
The TORT of acting carelessly towards someone to whom you have a duty of care, thereby causing them injury, loss or damage. It is the most wide-ranging tort, since the categories of potential negligence are not closed. Driving a car, giving professional advice, dry cleaning a suit, auditing a company; every activity of daily life involves doing something that may, if it is done carelessly, cause damage to someone else. The difficult question is what amounts to carelessness. The answer is focused on the duty of care: what duty, in all the circumstances of the case, was it reasonable to expect and did the DEFENDANT live up to it? If not, he was negligent. REASONABLENESS is a term of art and the test depends on an objective assessment of what a reasonable man would expect in those

circumstances. The principles of negligence were encapsulated in the 1932 LANDMARK decision of *Donoghue v Stevenson*, which involved someone finding a snail in a bottle of drink and suing the drinks company for negligence.

Lawyers and painters can soon change white to black.

Danish proverb

NEGOTIABLE INSTRUMENT
A bundle of rights encapsulated in a document that can be readily transferred from one person to another by the holder endorsing the document or an ancillary document that refers to it.

NEMINE CONTRADICENTE
More common in its abbreviated form *nem. con.*, this Latin maxim means "with no one speaking against" and is used to record a unanimous vote at a meeting.

NEMO DAT QUOD NON HABET
Known as the *nemo dat* rule, this Latin phrase means "no one can give what he does not have" and refers to a seller's inability to pass TITLE in property to a buyer if the seller does not own the property (because, for example, it is stolen). It does not seek to apportion any blame, since the seller may have innocently acquired the property from the thief, and the rule is often used to decide between two entirely innocent but competing claims to the same property.

NEXT FRIEND
A person who acts as a PLAINTIFF in LITIGATION on behalf of a MINOR.

NOLLE PROSEQUI
Latin for "do not pursue". An instruction to a court from the prosecuting authorities, in the UK usually from the ATTORNEY-GENERAL, not to proceed with a criminal trial.

NOMINAL CAPITAL

The total amount of EQUITY CAPITAL that a company may issue to its MEMBERS as set by its MEMORANDUM OF ASSOCIATION. It is also known as AUTHORISED CAPITAL, as distinct from ISSUED CAPITAL.

NOMINEE

Someone who is appointed to represent another. The legal relationship between the nominor and the nominee may be imprecise. It can amount to an AGENCY, where the nominee has defined authority to act on behalf of its PRINCIPAL, or it may be a BARE TRUST where the nominee merely holds a right on behalf of its nominor, such as a nominee shareholder who holds shares in trust for another (perhaps undisclosed) person.

The victim to too severe a law is considered as a martyr rather than a criminal.
Charles Caleb Colton, 1825

NON EST FACTUM

It is not his act or, perhaps, he did not mean to do it – in the sense that he did not know what he was doing. It is one of the rare cases where a court will overturn a seemingly binding CONTRACT by finding that one of the parties was sufficiently in the dark about what was going on that there was no meeting of the minds between them. The English case of *Lloyd's Bank v Bundy* is a fine example. At the request of his local bank manager an ageing, trusting farmer signed a sheaf of documents which created a MORTGAGE over his farm as SECURITY for a loan. The loan failed; the bank sought to enforce the security. Having heard the case, Lord Denning opened his judgement with words along the lines of "Old Farmer Bundy was an honest man" and everyone knew where the JUDGE's sympathies lay. It was a short step to establish that Mr Bundy had not understood the nature of the security documents and accordingly should not be bound by them. Non est factum, thank you very much.

NON-EXECUTIVE DIRECTOR

A company director who attends board meetings, gives advice to the company and carries all the potential liabilities of a director under the COMPANIES ACTS, but who does not work full-time for the company (as does an executive director). In recent times the rules for running a UK LISTED COMPANY have strengthened the role of non-executive directors. They are required to review the company's accounting procedures and to have a say in determining the remuneration of the executive directors and senior management. In VENTURE CAPITAL deals, a BUSINESS ANGEL will often take a role as a non-executive director.

NONSUIT

A situation arising in LITIGATION where a JUDGE determines that the PLAINTIFF has failed to establish a cause of action against the DEFENDANT, and accordingly the action has to be abandoned.

NOSCITUR A SOCIIS

"Let him be known by the society he keeps". More poetical than most Latin maxims that find their way into the law, this is a rule of legal construction (not far removed from EIUSDEM GENERIS) which determines that a general or ambiguous word should be given a more precise meaning by looking at the surrounding words and the particular context.

No law is quite appropriate for all.
Livy, 29 BC

NOTARY PUBLIC

In simple terms, a notary public is a lawyer who is officially authorised to witness documents, thereby anointing them with some form of official blessing. For example, documents required for the registration of rights in a foreign jurisdiction are often notarised (signed in the presence of and witnessed by a notary) so that the foreign authorities have the comfort of the notarial process in accepting the documents. There are two classes of notaries in England and Wales. A SCRIVENER NOTARY may practise throughout the country on the issue of a practising certificate by the Master of the Scriveners' Company. A GENERAL NOTARY (typically, a practising SOLICITOR who has taken this further qualification) may practise everywhere except within the jurisdiction of the Scriveners' Company, which is the City of London and a circuit of three miles surrounding the City. Sooner or later someone will suggest this exclusion smacks of monopolistic restraint, but with rules going back to 1373, no one is keen to attack the constitutional foundation of the Scriveners' Company.

NOT-FOR-PROFIT CORPORATION
A US term for a non-profit-making company, such as a quasi-governmental organisation or a charitable body.

NOTICE
To give someone notice of something or to serve a notice on someone is to let them know formally (usually in writing) of your intention to do something. Notice to quit is an intention to determine a LEASE and cease occupation of the premises. A termination notice is an intention to terminate a CONTRACT. The period of notice is the length of time required by the contract for giving notice. As a slightly different concept, to have notice of something means to be aware of it or have knowledge of it. (See the distinction between ACTUAL NOTICE and CONSTRUCTIVE NOTICE.)

NOT PROVEN
A term from Scottish law referring to a verdict of a criminal court that the DEFENDANT cannot be convicted because the prosecution failed to bring sufficient evidence to establish that he committed the alleged offence.

NOVATION
The formation of a new CONTRACT in place of an existing one, particularly where one party is re-

leased from the old contract and a new party is introduced in its place. Some contracts may be transferred by ASSIGNMENT, where the contractual right being transferred is a benefit, but in general you cannot assign the burden of a contract without the consent of the other party. For example, if I enter into a contract to tend your garden every week, I can assign to someone else the benefit (the payment for my services) but not the burden (the manual labour) without your consent. If you give your consent, it creates a new contract by novation. The old contract between you and me is replaced by a new one between you and the new gardener.

> *Justice is not a mincing-machine but a*
> *compromise.*
> Friedrich Dürrenmatt, 1952

NUISANCE

A TORT under COMMON LAW, private nuisance is the interference with someone's rights, usually relating to their quiet enjoyment of REAL ESTATE. Upsetting your neighbours with a noisy dog, a flood of water from your premises or late-night country and western music can be an unreasonable intrusion to their rights giving rise to an action for private nuisance. If the interference affects a number of people it may be a public nuisance, which is a criminal offence.

NULL AND VOID

If a CONTRACT is declared null and void, it has no force whatsoever and is treated as having never been formed in the first place.

NUNCUPATIVE WILL

An oral WILL made in the presence of a witness and accepted as valid only in the most extraordinary circumstances, such as one made by a dying solder on a battlefield.

OATH

A solemn declaration that what you are about to say (or write, in the case of an AFFIDAVIT) is the truth. The declaration is made while holding a bible or similar text relevant to your religion and by invoking the power of your chosen God. If you do not wish to swear by God, you can take an AFFIRMATION.

OBITER DICTA

Incidental comments. Part of a judgement delivered by a JUDGE at the end of a case which, although referring to the interpretation of a point of law, is not essential to his reasoning for reaching the decision and accordingly does not set a precedent at COMMON LAW for future interpretation. (Contrast with RATIO DECIDENDI.)

OBJECTS

The objects of a company are the purposes for which it is founded, for example, to carry on business as a trading company, a property development company and so on. The objects are recorded in its MEMORANDUM OF ASSOCIATION. They are distinguishable from a company's POWERS, which are also listed in the memorandum of association and must be exercised in conjunction with its objects.

OCCUPIER'S LIABILITY

The duty of an occupier of REAL ESTATE to make sure that the property does not cause harm or damage to visitors. This means making a dangerous structure safe, restraining a fierce dog or fencing a bottomless pit.

OFFER

An expression of willingness to enter into a CONTRACT. The contract is formed, provided there is CONSIDERATION and an evident intention by the parties to become legally bound, when the offer is accepted (see ACCEPTANCE).

OFFICE OF FAIR TRADING

A UK governmental agency that acts to protect the

interests of the public in business and consumer affairs.

Official Journal
Published in Brussels, the *Official Journal* contains the directives and regulations of the European Union.

Official receiver
A UK government official who is available to be appointed by a court to act as a liquidator of a company or a TRUSTEE IN BANKRUPTCY of a bankrupt person.

Official solicitor
A SOLICITOR who is available to be appointed to represent a MINOR or other person with a legal disability involved in LITIGATION in the HIGH COURT.

Old Bailey
The Central Criminal Court in London, UK.

Ombudsman
An official appointed to investigate complaints by the public against government departments or professional organisations. There are several ombudsmen in the UK: the Parliamentary Commissioner investigates complaints about abuse of governmental powers referred to him by a member of PARLIAMENT; the Legal Services Ombudsman investigates complaints against solicitors and barristers; the Banking Ombudsman deals with banks. An ombudsman does not hold any executive power. He will make recommendations to the department or organisation concerned (and may make his recommendations public) but he has no power to enforce them.

Open
Open correspondence between parties involved in LITIGATION is all correspondence between them that is not qualified as WITHOUT PREJUDICE. Open correspondence can be presented to the court as evidence; without prejudice correspondence cannot.

OPINION

See LEGAL OPINION.

Justice is impartiality. Only strangers are impartial.
George Bernard Shaw

OPTION

An opportunity, granted under and enforceable as a CONTRACT, for one party to require the other to buy or sell specified property. To be enforceable, the option must be exercised within a stated time or on the happening of a stated event, must clearly identify the property to be bought or sold and must specify a price or a workable price formula. A CALL OPTION is an option to buy; and a PUT OPTION is an option to sell.

ORDER IN COUNCIL

Most STATUTE law in the UK has to be considered and ratified by PARLIAMENT before it becomes effective. An exception is an Order in Council, which the government can introduce as LEGISLATION under powers delegated to it by an ACT OF PARLIAMENT. The order comes into force as law on receiving the ROYAL ASSENT and does not have to be ratified by Parliament.

ORDINANCE

In Hong Kong it is a STATUTE. In the USA it is a regulation issued by a municipal authority. In general, it is a decree or law issued by a governmental authority.

ORDINARY RESOLUTION

A resolution of the MEMBERS of a UK company passed by a simple majority of those voting, in contrast to a SPECIAL RESOLUTION, which must be passed by a 75% majority.

ORDINARY SHARE

The basic, standard SHARE of a company with straightforward voting rights and entitlements to dividends, as opposed to a share carrying customised rights such as a PREFERENCE SHARE.

ORIGINATING SUMMONS
A type of WRIT, this is a document which commences proceedings in certain actions in the HIGH COURT in England and Wales. An originating application is a similar document for starting certain actions in the COUNTY COURT.

OSTENSIBLE AUTHORITY
If someone appears to have authority to act on behalf of another because the other holds him out as having authority, such as a company giving an employee a title that includes the word DIRECTOR, you can enter into a binding CONTRACT with the company in reliance on that person's ostensible authority (whether or not he does in fact have authority).

There is a justice, but we do not always see it.
Discreet, smiling, it is there, at one side, a little
behind injustice, which makes a big noise.
Jules Renard, 1906

OUTSIDE DIRECTOR
Another term for a NON-EXECUTIVE DIRECTOR.

OVERREACHING
The concept of looking beyond an interest in property to the monetary value of the property as if it were sold. If a MORTGAGE entitles a mortgagee to take possession of charged property for the purpose of selling it, and entitles it to apply the sale proceeds against the reduction of the debt owed, the mortgagee has an overreaching interest in the sale proceeds.

OWNER-MANAGED
An owner-managed company is one where its directors are also its shareholders.

PALIMONY

Regular payments that a court orders a man to make to a woman (or, theoretically but rarely, vice versa) with whom he has been cohabiting but from whom he has now separated. The man and woman need not be husband and wife. In the USA it is also known as alimony. In the UK it is more commonly called maintenance payments.

PARALEGAL

A US term to describe an unqualified hired hand in a lawyer's office. It has evolved in general usage to cover a variety of situations. Most paralegals have some legal training, perhaps a law degree but not a professional qualification, and many are presented to clients as lawyers. Their attraction for a law firm is a reasonable understanding of the law and a cheap salary. A paralegal should not be confused with a LEGAL EXECUTIVE.

PARI PASSU

Latin for "of equal power", meaning there is no difference in the standing of two comparables. For example, if a company issues new shares with the same rights as existing shares, they are said to rank *pari passu*.

PARLIAMENT

The legislative body that makes the laws (statutes) of a country. In the USA it is called CONGRESS. In the UK Parliament consists of the House of Commons (lower house), the House of Lords (upper house) and the sovereign (in so far as the king or queen must give the ROYAL ASSENT to a STATUTE before it becomes law). Members of Parliament (MPS) are elected to the House of Commons, with the majority party forming the government of the day. The House of Lords is made up of hereditary peers (those who inherited their titles and positions), life peers (given their status for life by a government, usually as a reward for political service) and a motley crew of senior lawyers and bishops. Somewhat surprisingly, this hit and miss structure has been followed in other jurisdictions around the world (apart from the illogical and difficult concept of hereditary peers), to the extent that the UK system is known as the Mother of Parliaments (at least to those who sit within it). As prospective LEGISLATION travels through Parliament, it is known as a BILL. When it reaches its destination and becomes law, it is called an ACT OF PARLIAMENT.

> *In matters of government, justice means force as well as virtue.*
> Napoleon

PAROL
Parol evidence is evidence given orally to a court, with the witness attending in person, as opposed to written evidence, which is presented in an AFFIDAVIT.

PARTICULARS OF CLAIM
Details of a PLAINTIFF's claim as set out in the PLEADINGS put before a COUNTY COURT. In the HIGH COURT it is called a STATEMENT OF CLAIM. A request for further and better particulars is a formal step in the pleadings whereby one party asks the other for more information or details about its claim (or its defence).

PARTNERSHIP
Two or more people joining together for a common business purpose, and agreeing to share profits and losses between them, become a partnership. It requires no more formality than that. There is no need for a written agreement. There are no registration requirements. It is open to the partners to agree to share the profits or losses equally or in different proportions. From an outsider's viewpoint, however, all partners have JOINT and SEVERAL LIABILITY for the debts of the partnership. At present the professional bodies of most lawyers and accountants around the world require them to trade as partnerships rather than as corporations. This can expose individual partners to

massive liabilities, particularly accountants facing responsibility for an ill-judged audit of a large company, and there is considerable pressure to allow professional partnerships to incorporate or otherwise enjoy some measure of limited LIABILITY.

PART PERFORMANCE

This describes the situation where a party to a CONTRACT has performed some, but not all, of his obligations under the contract. Part performance can signify ACCEPTANCE of an OFFER and the creation of a contract. If by his conduct someone has started performing the contractual obligations, he cannot deny that a contract has been formed. For example, if a merchant receives an order for three consignments of beans and delivers the first one, he cannot later reject the contract or seek to avoid delivering the other two consignments. His part performance has confirmed the contract.

PAR VALUE

The face value of shares or STOCK, regardless of their issue price (as they may be issued at a premium above their par value) or their market value (as they may be trading at a premium or a discount to their par value). If a company has NOMINAL CAPITAL of £100,000 divided into 100,000 ordinary shares, the par value of each share is £1.

PASSING OFF

A TORT; passing off is dressing up your goods or services to suggest that they are connected with another, perhaps more established or more reputable, brand. It is an attempt to trade on another's reputation and is actionable by that person. A passing off action is often pursued in conjunction with a TRADE MARK action, since where a trader infringes another's trade mark, he is frequently attempting to pass off his goods (bearing the infringing trade mark) as those of the other trader. There are many infamous examples of deliberately mis-named goods seeking to replicate the real thing: Rolex watches, Christian Diorr garments, Luis Vutton leatherware and so on. There are also other, less obvious, attempts to trade on the back of someone else's reputation. The Coca Cola Company spends a lot of time and money in objecting to the production of rival drinks that, although bearing a different name, are marketed with its distinctive red and white livery.

A legal broom's a moral chimney-sweeper. And that's the reason he himself's so dirty.
Byron, *Don Juan*

PATENT

Formal recognition of a person's right to make and exploit an invention. A patent is recognised as an international right, enforceable around the world by a series of inter-country treaties, attaching to an invention. The international treaties, known as conventions, become part of the national law of the participating countries and allow patent rights to be enforced in their local courts. A successful patent registration depends on a careful and precise specification of the invention. There are many disputes based on a minor deviation to the design of a competing product which is claimed to circumvent its patent registration. A patent LICENCE is an agreement by a patent owner to allow someone to exploit the patent, usually in return for a ROYALTY.

PAYMENT IN

Apart from offending the rules of good grammar, a payment in (meaning a payment into court) can be a clever tactic for a DEFENDANT in UK court proceedings. A payment in is an offer of settlement. The defendant pays the offered sum to the court and the PLAINTIFF can withdraw it in full and final settlement of his claim. If he does not accept it, and the matter proceeds to trial where he fails to recover more than the amount paid in, the plaintiff has to pay the defendant's costs incurred since the date of the payment in. The skill, of course, is judging the amount to pay in – a pound too little will ruin the whole strategy.

PEPPERCORN

An example of where CONSIDERATION must be present but does not have to be adequate. A CONTRACT may provide for one party to pay a peppercorn in consideration for the other's obligations, such as a tenant paying a peppercorn rent to his landlord under a LEASE. Although it is purely nominal, the contract would be unenforceable without it.

A horse! A horse! My kingdom for a horse!
Richard III, through the pen of William Shakespeare, providing a fine example of where consideration would be sufficient for the law, although not necessarily adequate in economic terms

---

PERFORMING RIGHT

A LICENCE to allow someone to play music or perform drama that is protected by COPYRIGHT.

PERIODIC TENANCY

A LEASE of REAL ESTATE for successive periods, say monthly, rather than for a fixed length of time.

PERSONALTY

Personal property, such as goods and chattels, as opposed to REAL ESTATE.

PETITION

Any type of application to a court seeking a remedy or relief, as in a WINDING UP petition, a BANKRUPTCY petition or a divorce petition.

PLAINTIFF

The person who initiates the proceedings (that is, files the suit or issues the WRIT) in LITIGATION. The person must have legal personality, which means the PLAINTIFF must be a living person, a PARTNERSHIP or a properly constituted corporation (including a public body). The word is derived from plaint, meaning a claim.

PLEADINGS

The bundle of formal papers lodged with a court

by each side to set out its case. The bundle expands gradually as the action proceeds. In the HIGH COURT it starts with the WRIT and the STATEMENT OF CLAIM, followed by the ACKNOWLEDGEMENT OF SERVICE, then the DEFENCE, then further and better particulars, then amendments and so on.

PLEDGE

To hand over possession (but not ownership) of an object or chattel as SECURITY for a debt (for example, to a pawnbroker); a type of equitable CHARGE or MORTGAGE.

Law suits consume time, money, rest and friends.
George Herbert, 1640

PLUM

In MERGERS AND ACQUISITIONS jargon, a plum is a good deal or an attractive investment. In sharp contrast to a LEMON, this fruit is a pleasure to get your teeth into.

POLL

When the MEMBERS of a company come to vote on a resolution at a GENERAL MEETING they may do so on a show of hands (being one vote for every member present at the meeting), or alternatively someone may call for a poll. Conducted as a ballot, a poll gives shareholders one vote for each SHARE they hold, and the resolution will be decided according to the will of the majority shareholders, not necessarily the majority of the individuals at the meeting.

POSSESSORY TITLE

Acquiring ownership through squatter's rights (see ADVERSE POSSESSION). If you occupy land for long enough (say, 12 years) without complaint from the true owner (if there is one), you can acquire legal ownership.

POST OBIT BOND

A bastardised Latin expression, twisted to describe

---

a loan or other arrangement where you acknowledge a debt and agree to repay it from money you expect to receive as a LEGACY under someone's WILL.

POWER OF APPOINTMENT

Power given to a person, usually a TRUSTEE by virtue of the powers set out in the TRUST deed, to dispose of property that belongs to someone else, such as the property forming part of the trust fund.

POWER OF ATTORNEY

Formal authority for someone to act on behalf of someone else. The scope of the power depends on the language used in the document that records it. It can be a general power, as in the UK where a document refers to the general scope of section 10 of the Powers of Attorney Act, which allows the attorney to do everything that the person on whose authority he is acting could lawfully do. Alternatively, it can be a specific power where the document records the extent of the attorney's power, say to execute and deliver a specified CONTRACT. Apart from construing the scope, another issue is how long a power of attorney will last. It is fine if it records a definite time period, but many are indefinite, and a third party cannot tell whether or not the donor has revoked it. Legal systems are forced to come up with arbitrary rules, such as saying that a third party should not necessarily rely on a power of attorney more than a year old without confirming that it is still valid.

> *Justice is the right of the weakest.*
> Joseph Joubert, 1842

POWERS

The powers of a company are set out, together with its OBJECTS, in its MEMORANDUM OF ASSOCIATION. They act as confirmation to outsiders that the company has power to do things, such as to grant SECURITY or give guarantees, provided they are exercised in conjunction with and for the purposes of the objects.

PRACTICE DIRECTION
A ruling issued by a JUDGE on how a court procedure should be carried out.

PRACTICE MASTER
A JUDGE who sits in the HIGH COURT in London to hear submissions from litigants (usually through their solicitors) without appointments and will give directions on how their actions should be conducted. For example, the practice master may give a DEFENDANT more time to submit his defence than is supposedly allowed by the rules of the WHITE BOOK.

PRAECIPE
Not a legal recipe, but a formal request to a court asking for the approval and issue of a specified document, such as the issue of a SUBPOENA to a prospective witness.

PRAY
What lawyers, particularly barristers, do in court when the JUDGE appears to give little credence to their arguments, as in: "My lord, I pray in aid the authority of ..."

PREAMBLE
The introductory words in a CONTRACT, BILL or STATUTE that describe the main theme but do not form part of the substantive content. In a traditional contract, the preamble starts with the word "whereas".

PRECATORY
The precatory words in a WILL are those that request something to be done, as in "please scatter my ashes at Sloppy Joe's Bar and Grill".

PRE-EMPTION
A formal right of first refusal. It is common for the ARTICLES OF ASSOCIATION of a UK PRIVATE COMPANY to

contain pre-emption rights whereby any share-holder wishing to sell its shares must offer them to the other shareholders before selling them to an outsider. Similarly, the COMPANIES ACTS require a UK company to offer new shares to its existing shareholders before issuing them to an outsider.

> *Wherever law ends, tyranny begins.*
> John Locke, 1690

PREFERENCE SHARE

All shares are equal, but some shares are more equal than others. The rights attaching to a company's shares are set out in its ARTICLES OF ASSOCIATION and they can vary from one class of shares to another. The most common variations are the ranking for dividends on the distribution of profits and the ranking for the distribution of assets on a WINDING UP. Preference shares can have various forms, but they usually carry a right to receive a stated dividend (expressed as a percentage of their PAR VALUE) before any other (usually the ordinary) shares. With a priority in receiving dividends, preference shares will often have reduced rights in other areas, such as no voting rights or no entitlement to share in the distribution of assets in a winding up. In this way they can be used as a corporate finance tool, as a hybrid type of financing, somewhere between DEBT FINANCE and EQUITY CAPITAL.

PREFERENTIAL CREDITOR

A preferential (or preferred) creditor is one who must be paid first in a company's LIQUIDATION, such as a secured creditor or the Inland Revenue, in preference to the general (unsecured) creditors.

PRESCRIPTION

Not only something you take to the pharmacy, but a right you acquire over a period of time, such as a right of ownership to REAL ESTATE acquired by ADVERSE POSSESSION.

PRESENTS

A word, which should be avoided, used to mean "this document".

PRE-TRIAL REVIEW

A meeting of the parties involved in LITIGATION, usually under the auspices of a JUDGE or court official, to discuss the mechanics of the trial. The aim is to streamline the trial process by focusing on the relevant issues. For example, the judge may ask each side to submit skeleton arguments before the hearing starts. The parties may agree to accept selected witness statements to avoid the need for some witnesses to attend court. If there is little agreement or co-operation between them, they will at least work out which evidential documents they want to bring to court so that a complete set may be assembled.

PRICE FIXING

An unlawful agreement between two parties, usually two suppliers or a supplier and a distributor, to charge an agreed price for goods that otherwise would be subject to competitive forces. Price fixing is anti-competitive and distorts free trade. In Europe it is unlawful under the TREATY OF ROME; in the USA it is contrary to ANTI-TRUST LEGISLATION.

PRIMA FACIE

Latin for "on the face of it". If a DEFENDANT can show that he has a *prima facie* defence to an action, where a court recognises that his arguments look valid at face value (without any investigation of the facts or testing of the arguments), he should be able to resist a PLAINTIFF's application for SUMMARY JUDGEMENT and have the action heard at a full trial. Similarly, in COMMITTAL PROCEEDINGS, the prosecutor has to show that there is a *prima facie* case to answer before the prosecution can go forward to a full trial.

PRIMARY EVIDENCE

Evidence presented to a court by a witness with first-hand knowledge of the facts, as opposed to

HEARSAY EVIDENCE, which is merely recounting what someone else said happened.

Justice should remove the bandage from her eyes long enough to distinguish between the vicious and the unfortunate.
Robert G. Ingersoll, 1884

PRIMOGENITURE
A harsh rule of inheritance adopted by archaic legal systems whereby the eldest son gets the lot.

PRINCIPAL
The main protagonist in a commercial transaction. An agent (see AGENCY) acts on behalf of a principal; a CONTRACT may be negotiated by an agent, but the contracting party will be the principal.

PRIVACY
The law has difficulty in dealing with this concept. Some jurisdictions, specially in continental Europe, have tried to legislate to protect an individual's right to lead a private life without being exposed to public scrutiny, particularly by salacious revelations in the press. Other jurisdictions, including the UK, have so far shied away from legislating against the invasion of privacy. The problem is to lay down rules of general application, which need to cover vastly differing circumstances. Many people agree that a celebrity's sexual peccadilloes should be a private matter (within bounds, perhaps, but this is already hinting at the difficulty of achieving a consensus in this area) most would also agree that it is beneficial to have a free press that can expose corruption in the private lives of public officials. The USA faces the problem from this latter viewpoint. Spurred by bad experiences at the hands of a meddlesome government across the Atlantic, the fathers of American independence introduced the right of free speech as the First Amendment to the US Constitution. This gives newspapers a right to publish what they believe to be the truth, with scant regard for the pri-

vacy of individuals. Because it is difficult to
achieve a balance between these competing
rights, many legislators fear to try.

PRIVATE COMPANY
According to the COMPANIES ACTS there are three
defining characteristics of a UK private company.

- It cannot offer its shares to the public; there
  are a hatful of cases on what constitutes the
  public, but it is not always clear cut.
- Transfers of its shares are controlled by its
  directors, who can refuse to register a
  transfer to someone they do not like.
- It usually has a restriction (in its ARTICLES OF
  ASSOCIATION) of a maximum of 50
  shareholders at any one time, although this
  restriction can be lifted and the company
  will remain a private company.

PRIVILEGE
Protection from LIABILITY in specified circumstances, such as a defence against an action for
DEFAMATION. Absolute privilege protects you from
being sued for defamation if you are an MP making a statement in PARLIAMENT or a lawyer presenting a case in court. Qualified privilege protects
you where you can show that a defamatory statement was made without malice. A privileged communication is a statement that cannot be used
against you in court, such as a communication between you and your lawyer.

PRIVITY OF CONTRACT
This fundamental principle of CONTRACT law requires that you can claim a benefit under a contract only if you are a party to the contract. Merely
being mentioned by the other parties may not be
enough to secure an enforceable right; but in general you are out of the reckoning if you are not a
party to the contract.

PRIVY COUNCIL
The Judicial Committee of the Privy Council,

which is made up of senior judges who invariably sit on the Judicial Committee of the House of Lords, is the final court of APPEAL for jurisdictions outside the UK that choose to use the UK legal system, such as UK colonies and some members of the Commonwealth.

The first thing we do, let's kill all the lawyers.
William Shakespeare, *Henry IV, Part II*

PROBATE
Legal acknowledgement that a WILL is valid. It is issued by the court to the executors named in the will and serves as formal authorisation of their power to implement the terms of the will and to act as the legal representatives of the deceased person's estate.

PROCESS-SERVER
Someone who delivers a legal document, such as a WRIT, to the designated addressee by way of SERVICE OF PROCESS.

PROCURATOR FISCAL
A law officer in SCOTLAND who decides whether or not to start a criminal prosecution against an alleged criminal.

PROFIT PRENDRE
Another expression the law seems to think is useful. Profit prendre refers to the right to take fish or game from someone's land.

Useless laws weaken necessary ones.
Montesquieu, 1748

PROMISSORY ESTOPPEL
An extension to the doctrine of ESTOPPEL (one of the rules of EQUITY). Promissory estoppel prevents someone from denying the fulfilment of a promise he has made to someone else where the other has relied on that promise and acted to his detriment

as a result. For example, if a retailer says to a wholesaler "If you buy 1,000 bales of hay, I will buy 600 of them from you" and subsequently refuses to accept delivery, denying that it had made any CONTRACT to purchase the hay, the wholesaler may have an action against the retailer based on promissory estoppel. In this way, although there is no contract formed under the strict rules of COMMON LAW, a court is able to do justice by imputing the more flexible rules of equity.

PROMISSORY NOTE
A grandiose term for something really simple. It is nothing more than a written acknowledgement of a debt in its simplest form: an IOU. It can be blown up to look like a sophisticated investment tool, as in the case of a JUNK BOND, but this is for the sake of marketing securities to unwary investors rather than compliance with legal principles. The most familiar form of a promissory note is a bank note used as common currency; it merely confirms that the issuer (in the UK, the Bank of England) will pay the bearer the sum recorded in the note.

PROOF OF DEBT
To prove a debt means to take action to claim a payment due to you from a bankrupt person or a company in LIQUIDATION.

PROPER LAW
The proper law of a CONTRACT is the law of a particular jurisdiction which the parties agree should govern the contract or, in the absence of agreement, which the rules of law so determine. As different jurisdictions have different rules, the parties may need to resolve this as an issue preliminary to the main issue.

PROPRIETARY COMPANY
In jurisdictions such as Australia and South Africa, a proprietary company is the equivalent of a PRIVATE COMPANY. It is usually designated by the abbreviation Pty.

PROSPECTUS

A document issued to the public giving information about a company that is to be floated on a stock exchange. In the UK the contents of a prospectus are dictated by the Yellow Book (the Rules for the Admission of Securities to the Official List of the London Stock Exchange) and the COMPANIES ACTS.

Laws too gentle are seldom obeyed; too severe, seldom executed.
Benjamin Franklin, 1732

PROXY

An appointment to act on behalf of someone else, particularly to vote on behalf of a shareholder at a GENERAL MEETING of a company.

PUBLIC COMPANY

A public company is a company whose shares are owned by the public. Well, it is sometimes, but not always. A public limited company (or PLC or Plc or plc) may be a LISTED COMPANY and have its shares listed on a stock exchange (see FLOTATION) to make them available to the public. A public company can be contrasted with a PRIVATE COMPANY, which is not allowed to offer its shares to the public. However, there are plenty of companies in the UK labelled PLC that are public companies but not listed companies. They have the constitution of a public company without the restrictions of a private company in their ARTICLES OF ASSOCIATION, but they have the structure of a private company, for example, with a few shareholders who are often their managers. The conclusion that such companies are seeking to enhance their status by wearing fancy clothes would be ungenerous.

PUNITIVE DAMAGES

DAMAGES awarded to a PLAINTIFF over and above the actual loss suffered. As this is not strictly compensation, it is a sign that the court wishes to punish the DEFENDANT for acting badly towards the plaintiff. Also known as exemplary damages, punitive damages are often awarded in DEFAMATION actions where it is difficult for a court to assess the actual loss suffered as a result of a malicious slur on someone's character.

PUPILLAGE

A form of apprenticeship for someone training to be a BARRISTER. Having passed the necessary examinations you can be called to the bar (that is, admitted as a qualified barrister at one of the INNS OF COURT), but you cannot practise until you have done pupillage. This means attaching yourself to an experienced barrister for six months (usually followed by a second six months, possibly with another barrister) in the hope that you will pick up some of the tricks of the trade as you go along.

PUT OPTION

A contractual right to require someone to buy something, such as SHARES, from you. The CONTRACT usually indicates a period of time during which the OPTION may be exercised (the option period) and a mechanism to determine the price to be paid (the option price). The reverse of a put option, namely the right to require someone to sell something to you, is a CALL OPTION.

Q

QC
See QUEEN'S COUNSEL.

QUALIFIED AUDIT REPORT
In US parlance, a qualified opinion. This is a report by a company's auditors on its FINANCIAL STATEMENTS (accounts) where they do not feel able to certify that the statements comply with generally accepted accounting principles in all respects. The reason for the qualification will be given in the audit report and may refer to a restriction on the scope of their investigation or a failure to agree with the conclusions reached by the company's management. Any qualification will be closely examined by the company's shareholders when the accounts are presented to them.

QUALIFIED TITLE
TITLE to property, particularly REAL ESTATE, which is not absolute (unimpeachable) because of some defect or competing claim.

QUANTUM MERUIT
Latin for "as much as he deserves". This expression gives a name to an action where someone claims payment for the amount of work he has done for someone else, particularly where he cannot claim under a CONTRACT. For example, if you hire someone to build a wall in your garden and he builds only half of it before your garden is engulfed by an unaccountable rise in the water level of your neighbouring lake (thereby rendering further work impossible and your contract NULL AND VOID by virtue of FRUSTRATION), your builder may well have a *quantum meruit* claim against you for the amount of work he actually did perform.

QUARTER DAY
The four days each year when, traditionally, rents are paid for the possession of land. The days are March 25th (Lady Day), June 24th (Midsummer Day), September 29th (Michaelmas Day) and December 25th (Christmas Day).

QUEEN'S BENCH DIVISION

One of the three divisions of the HIGH COURT. The Queen's Bench Division deals with general civil claims, that is, those that do not fall within the scope of the CHANCERY DIVISION or of the FAMILY DIVISION.

QUEEN'S COUNSEL

A senior BARRISTER who (after unselfishly allowing his name to be put forward) has accepted the invitation of the LORD CHANCELLOR to join the upper ranks of the profession by taking silk, that is, forswears the common-or-garden cotton gown for an altogether smarter, silk version. As a result of this increased expenditure on work attire, the fees a Queen's Counsel (QC) commands will double overnight. The name changes to King's Counsel (KC) if the monarch is male.

> *I do not care to speak ill of any man behind his back, but I believe this man is an attorney.*
> Samuel Johnson

QUIET ENJOYMENT

The basic right a landlord gives to a tenant under a LEASE, namely the right to occupy the property without interference and without anyone claiming any conflicting rights.

RACK RENT
Full market rent for REAL ESTATE under a LEASE.

RATCHET
A device used in MANAGEMENT BUY-OUT transactions to give the management team an incentive to meet ambitious targets. It is incorporated in the agreement between the managers and the provider of VENTURE CAPITAL and allows the managers to get a proportionally larger share of the EQUITY CAPITAL of the company (that is, to ratchet up their investment) if the company achieves agreed targets.

RATIO DECIDENDI
Latin for "the reason for deciding". As opposed to OBITER DICTA, the *ratio decidendi* is the main part of a JUDGE's reasoning in deciding a case, the part that examines the relevant legal principles and applies them to the particular circumstances, thereby setting a precedent which other courts must follow. Often abbreviated to *ratio*, the concept of sorting the wheat (the vital reasoning) from the chaff (the incidental comments) is fundamental to the COMMON LAW system, which relies on the application of precedent.

REAL ESTATE
Real estate, as opposed to personal estate, is a right *in rem*, a Latin term meaning "in respect of the thing". Personal estate is a right *in personam*, meaning "in respect of the person". The law recognises that some property – land and buildings – is sufficiently important to have its own recognised standing at law. This is real estate. Other property, such as a personal chattel, is recognised at law only according to the claims of the person who owns it. This is personal estate. A realtor is a US term for someone who deals in or brokers real estate.

REASONABLENESS
An objective standard of rational behaviour. Every legal system has to set a yardstick against which alleged wrongs can be judged. The CIVIL LAW sys-

tem of continental Europe makes much of the quality of GOOD FAITH. The COMMON LAW system relies more on the concept of reasonableness and the estimation of how a reasonable man (it does not seem to anticipate the possibility that there might be a reasonable woman) would have reacted in the given circumstances. Particularly in the TORT of NEGLIGENCE, this imaginary character of average intelligence and calm disposition is continually thrust forward as the yardstick of acceptable social behaviour. At the root of the concept is the distinction between subjective and objective judgement. The DEFENDANT, being an accomplished racing driver, may sincerely believe he is safe to drive at 75mph through city streets; the more objective view of the reasonable man, who is neither too reckless nor too timid, is that such driving is dangerous and foolhardy. The reasonable man is the ordinary man in the street or (as English jurisprudence would have it) the man riding on a Clapham omnibus.

> *The Common Law of England has been laboriously built about a mythical figure – the figure of "The Reasonable Man".*
> A. P. Herbert, 1935

RECEIVER

A person appointed by a creditor, or a court on the application of a creditor, to administer the affairs of a debtor company and to liquidate its assets until it has paid the debt owed to the creditor. Typically, a receiver (usually an accountant or a professional insolvency practitioner) is appointed by a bank under powers granted by a MORTGAGE, CHARGE or other SECURITY given to the bank by the company on obtaining loan facilities. Without a contractual power to appoint a receiver, the creditor must apply to the court for one to be appointed. If the company is in good health, the receiver may be discharged once the debt is paid and life will go on, but frequently receivership leads to LIQUIDATION and the end of the road.

RECIPROCAL HOLDINGS
An arrangement between two companies whereby each holds shares in the other with a view to fending off unwanted takeovers. Inevitably, if one succumbs to a takeover the other is immediately threatened (in stockmarket jargon, it is in play).

RECORDER
A part-time judge in the Crown Court. The position is often taken by a working BARRISTER in preparation for a permanent judicial role.

RECOVERY FINANCE
An investment in a company that is in some financial difficulty where the investor, usually a VENTURE CAPITAL provider, sees an opportunity to turn its fortunes around. Recovery finance can take many forms, either as EQUITY CAPITAL or DEBT FINANCE.

REDEEMABLE
Something that can be surrendered for cash. Redeemable shares are shares which the shareholder can surrender to the company for cash or which the company can buy back from the shareholder. Under current English law only preference shares may be issued with redemption rights; the surrender of ordinary shares for cash must be authorised by the court as a reduction of capital.

REDUNDANCY
Termination of employment on the ground that the job no longer exists or is no longer necessary. The closure of a business will inevitably result in employees being made redundant, but there are many other, less clear examples. A change in business practice, the introduction of new technology or a restructuring of a department may lead to surplus job positions. Most western jurisdictions require an employer to pay compensation to any employee made redundant, usually calculated on the employee's length of service. Voluntary redundancy is where an employer invites members of its workforce to accept an enhanced com-

pensation package rather than face the risk of selection for compulsory redundancy and minimum compensation. (For a commonly used selection policy, see LAST IN, FIRST OUT.)

REFINANCING

A refinancing usually means that a company is in financial difficulty and needs an injection of new funds to restore it to financial health, but it may mean that the company is doing sufficiently well that its management can refinance the business on more favourable terms than it currently enjoys. This is often the aim of a team of managers in a MANAGEMENT BUY-OUT, where they use the resources of one VENTURE CAPITAL provider to finance the buy-out but seek to refinance with another on better terms as soon as their business allows.

REFRESHER

The daily fee paid to a BARRISTER for the second and subsequent days of a trial. He gets a BRIEF fee for the preparatory work (such as reading the papers) and for appearing on the first day of the trial; thereafter he needs to be refreshed every day to get him to turn up.

REGINA

Latin for "the queen", meaning the Crown or the state when it is a party to legal proceedings. Like REX it is usually abbreviated to the initial letter, as in *R. v Smith*.

REGISTERED LAND

REAL ESTATE that has been registered with the LAND REGISTRY, so that the registered owner's TITLE is officially recognised. The register also contains details of any CHARGE, EASEMENT and other ENCUMBRANCE affecting the land.

REGISTERED OFFICE

The official address of a UK company, as registered with the REGISTRAR OF COMPANIES, where SERVICE OF PROCESS may take place.

REGISTRAR OF COMPANIES

The governmental official given the task of supervising the register of UK companies. Under the COMPANIES ACTS every company must provide designated information to the Registrar of Companies, who places it on public record for all to see (a COMPANY SEARCH). The registrar lives at COMPANIES HOUSE, of course.

REJOINDER

A riposte. In LITIGATION in the HIGH COURT the PLAINTIFF starts the ball rolling with a WRIT; the DEFENDANT replies with an ACKNOWLEDGEMENT OF SERVICE; the plaintiff proceeds with a STATEMENT OF CLAIM; the defendant answers with a defence; the plaintiff counters with a reply; and the defendant makes a riposte with a rejoinder.

RELATOR

Someone who makes a formal proposal to the ATTORNEY-GENERAL, as head of the UK criminal prosecution service, that proceedings should be brought against someone else. It is found in matters of ADMINISTRATIVE LAW where a private person urges the Crown (the State) to take legal action against a governmental or public body.

RELEASE AND DISCHARGE

When a debtor pays off a debt and the creditor accepts the payment in full and final settlement of its claim for the debt (see ACCORD AND SATISFACTION), the acknowledgement by the creditor is called a release and discharge of the debt. This signifies that the creditor has abandoned its right to sue the debtor for the debt and releases the debtor from it.

Further, 30 marks, for being awoken in the night and having thought over your case.
Extract from a German lawyer's bill

REMAINDER

An interest in remainder is a contingent owner-

R

ship right that will become an actual right only when someone else's interest has expired. For example, if you give your son the right to occupy a house during his lifetime (a LIFE INTEREST) and direct that after his death it should pass to your grandchildren, their interest will be an interest in remainder.

REMOTENESS OF DAMAGE

A defence to an action in LITIGATION where the DEFENDANT maintains that the loss or injury suffered by the PLAINTIFF could not reasonably have been foreseen from his actions and accordingly he should not be held liable for it. The defendant may admit that his action started the chain of events which ultimately led to the loss or injury, but it was too remote for him to be held responsible. This defence is less well developed in the USA where anyone who has the misfortune to be enmeshed in the chain of events is likely to be named in the WRIT and to face LIABILITY.

RENUNCIATION

Where a company embarks on a RIGHTS ISSUE or a similar exercise giving its shareholders the opportunity to acquire new shares, it will send every shareholder a bundle of papers explaining and presenting the offer. This bundle will usually include a letter of renunciation so that, if the shareholder does not want to take the shares himself, he can renounce his rights in favour of someone else and instruct the company to deliver the shares to that other person.

REPORTED CASE

The decision of a court case, including the JUDGE's reasoning, which is recorded and published in the LAW REPORTS because of its importance in setting a precedent that other courts must follow.

REPUDIATION

If you repudiate a CONTRACT, you refuse or fail to perform your contractual obligations. This may be express repudiation ("I am leaving and I am not

R

coming back") or merely implied by your conduct (failure to deliver on the specified date). Either way, the other party has a potential action against you for breach of contract.

REQUISITION ON TITLE

As a preliminary step in the transfer (see CON-VEYANCE) of REAL ESTATE, the seller's lawyer will send the buyer's lawyer details of the TITLE to the property. The buyer's lawyer will review these and investigate the title to satisfy himself that the seller does indeed own the property and that there are no competing claims. He may ask the seller's lawyer for more details; these requests are known as requisitions on title.

Laws grind the poor, and rich men rule the law.
Oliver Goldsmith, 1765

RESCISSION

A right of rescission gives a contracting party the right to cancel a CONTRACT without suffering any LIABILITY. This right can either be granted under the terms of the contract or may arise by operation of law. For example, the parties may agree as part of the contractual terms that if certain conditions are not fulfilled by a certain date any or one of them may pull out and cancel the contract. Similarly, there is a line of authority in CASE LAW which says that if there has been a breach of contract that is fundamental to the essence of the contract, the innocent party can claim a right of rescission and thereby claim the contract is NULL AND VOID. For example, if a shipbuilder delivers a finished ship that fundamentally differs from the agreed plans, the purchaser may be entitled to reject it and rescind the contract.

RESIDUE

The residue of an ESTATE (or the residuary estate) is that part of a deceased person's assets left over after his or her debts and bequests have been paid. It is used as a sweep-up category in a WILL:

"with the residue of my estate going to my nephew, Algernon".

RES IPSA LOQUITUR

A Latin phrase that translates as "it speaks for itself", meaning it is blindingly obvious. It is used in court-room arguments where one counsel maintains that the indisputable facts are sufficient to establish his client's case, thereby trying to force onto the other side the burden of proving that it is not so. Cynics may say that this tactic is used when a case is so weak that the counsel cannot think of any convincing argument to support it other than to say "it is so blindingly obvious that I am not going to go into any details".

"With all due respect…"

The words likely to preface a particularly disrespectful comment from an archetypal British barrister

---

RES JUDICATA

Another Latin phrase, meaning "something on which judgement has already been given". A court (unless it is an APPEAL COURT) cannot open up an issue that has already been decided by another court, and this little phrase is a reminder to lawyers not to try.

RESTITUTION

A LITIGATION action where you claim back something that has been wrongfully taken from you. If your car is stolen and the thief sells it to an innocent third party, you may have an action for restitution against the third party.

RESTRAINT OF TRADE

A CONTRACT, or a part of a contract, that has the effect of restricting the freedom of one party to carry on its business, particularly where it gives the other party some form of economic advantage. The contract may require a retailer to buy certain goods from only one supplier (a SOLUS AGREEMENT) or may contain a RESTRICTIVE COVENANT that a trader will not set up a competing business in a designated area for a specified time. Many such provisions are held to be unenforceable, either because they are contrary to ANTI-TRUST LEGISLATION or because the court considers them to be unreasonable in the circumstances, but others are accepted as exceptions to anti-trust rules on grounds of commercial necessity.

I regret to say that we of the FBI are powerless to act in cases of oral-genital intimacy, unless it has in some way obstructed interstate commerce.
J. Edgar Hoover

RESTRICTIVE COVENANT
A provision in a CONTRACT that prevents someone from doing something. It may stop the party disclosing trade secrets, enticing away someone else's employees or competing against another business.

RESTRICTIVE PRACTICES
An expression used in the UK to describe anti-competitive practices that restrict free competition in the supply of goods or services with a view to protecting the supplier's prices. The peculiar English law in this area has gradually been overtaken by EU competition law laid down by the TREATY OF ROME.

RETENTION OF TITLE
See ROMALPA CLAUSE.

REVERSION
The interest of a landlord in REAL ESTATE that is subject to a LEASE, meaning that the property will revert to the landlord at the end of the lease. If the landlord wants to dispose of his interest, he must assign the reversion to someone else. Obviously, the reversion becomes more valuable as the end of the lease gets nearer. A reversion is not quite the same as a reversionary interest, which, like a REMAINDER, suggests the transfer of property from

one owner to another on the death of the first owner.

REVOCATION
The act of cancelling or annulling something, perhaps a CONTRACT, a LICENCE or a WILL, where you have a right to do so. You cannot revoke a contract unless you have the appropriate power under its terms; if you do not have power, you will be in breach of the contract by virtue of your REPUDIATION. You might claim this power as a result of the other party's breach, by seeking to revoke its rights under the contract because it has not fulfilled its obligations.

REX
Latin for "the king", meaning the Crown or the state when it is a party to legal proceedings. Like REGINA it is usually abbreviated to the (conveniently identical) initial letter, as in *R. v Smith*.

RIDER
An additional clause to a CONTRACT (or in legislative terms a BILL) which is inserted as an amendment to the current draft.

RIGHTS ISSUE
An offer by a company to its shareholders to subscribe for some new shares, often at a discount to the market price, in proportion to the number of shares they currently hold. A BONUS ISSUE gives away the new shares, without requiring any payment, by capitalising the accumulated reserves (profits) of the company.

RIPARIAN RIGHTS
Fishing rights or other rights of an owner of land adjoining a river.

RISK
The chance or likelihood of suffering loss, damage or LIABILITY and the corresponding responsibility for it. Risk permeates every aspect of commercial law. When you buy something there

are two components in the transfer of legal rights associated with the purchase: TITLE and risk. Title represents the ownership rights and risk represents the responsibility for any liability attaching to the object transferred. When you enter into a CONTRACT the risk is the chance that you will be unable to perform your obligations, thereby leaving yourself open to liability to the other party for breach of contract.

ROMALPA CLAUSE

Taken from the name of a significant UK case on the topic, a Romalpa clause is also known as a RETENTION OF TITLE clause. It is found in the better drafted terms of sale (often in standard terms printed on the back of a supplier's order forms) and is a device whereby a seller seeks to retain TITLE to goods sold and delivered to a buyer until payment of the purchase price is made. The aim is to protect the seller in the event of the buyer's insolvency. If the buyer goes bust before payment has been made, the seller can claim back the goods on the ground that title has not passed. If title had passed, the buyer's TRUSTEE IN BANKRUPTCY, liquidator, RECEIVER, or whoever could claim the goods and the seller would be left to chase after payment of the purchase price in a line of unsecured creditors. It is better to get the goods back if you can. Problems start, of course, where the seller's goods (such as raw materials) have been put through a manufacturing process or mixed with goods from another supplier. It is one thing to reclaim title over a clearly identified stack of timber in the buyer's warehouse, but quite another to argue over a finished wardrobe in the showroom. The courts have tried, with varying success, to lay down workable rules but arguments between suppliers and receivers over retention of title clauses are inevitable.

ROMAN LAW

The system of laws established across Europe at the time of the Roman Empire. It remains a characteristic part of the CIVIL LAW system adopted by many continental European jurisdictions, but has little influence on the COMMON LAW system established under English law.

Good laws lead to the making of better ones; bad ones bring out the worse.
Jean-Jacques Rousseau, 1762

ROOT OF TITLE

An expression used to describe a fundamental concept in conveyancing law. The root of title is the original document that establishes TITLE (ownership) to a parcel of land and thereby provides reliable evidence that the seller has the necessary right to sell the land. For REGISTERED LAND in the UK, the root of the title is the LAND CERTIFICATE. For unregistered land, the conveyancer may have to trace the line of uninterrupted and reliable documents to prove the seller's ownership rights.

ROYAL ASSENT

The final stage in the process of passing LEGISLATION through PARLIAMENT in the UK. Draft legislation in the form of a BILL is presented to, debated in and passed by the House of Commons and then the House of Lords. Thereafter, in its final form, it is sent to the monarch for the Royal Assent. This action by the sovereign is the formality to signify the end of the parliamentary process.

ROYAL PREROGATIVE

Any special right or power exercised exclusively by the monarch, such as the UK queen's (or king's) right to dissolve PARLIAMENT and call a general election.

ROYALTY

Money paid in return for exercising a right under a LICENCE. Thus a publisher pays a royalty to an author for the right to publish his work under a COPYRIGHT licence. Royalties are usually calculated as a percentage of the earnings received from exploitation of the licensed rights, so that the publisher's and author's interests are tied together with the aim of maximising sales for the benefit of both. Authors normally receive an advance against royalties as part of the contract to exploit the work. Successful authors, with powerful agents, have been known to secure advances that have far exceeded the royalties they would have received in the end.

RYLANDS V. FLETCHER

This famous case established a useful rule of English REAL ESTATE law. If someone brings something (such as a dangerous substance or an animal) onto his land and it escapes, causing damage to a neighbour's property, he bears LIABILITY for that damage (without the injured party having to prove NEGLIGENCE) and must pay compensation to his neighbour.

Rigid justice is the greatest injustice.
Thomas Fuller, 1732

SALE AND LEASE BACK

A convoluted transaction where the owner of REAL ESTATE sells the FREEHOLD interest to someone and simultaneously takes a LEASE back from the new owner. He therefore remains in occupation of the land, but has changed (downgraded) his legal interest and has pocketed a capital sum in return for his agreement to pay rent. The mechanism can also be applied where someone sells a long-term leasehold interest and takes back a shorter lease.

SALE OR RETURN

A transaction whereby a manufacturer or a supplier delivers goods to a retailer on the understanding that the retailer may return them, without paying the purchase price, if they are unsold within a certain time. The legal analysis is this: the supplier retains TITLE to the goods, but allows the retailer to take possession of them (under a form of BAILMENT) for the purpose of finding a buyer. At the point of sale to a customer, title is transferred from the supplier to the retailer and on to the customer. If the goods are unsold, they are simply returned to the supplier, who has retained the title to them throughout their circuitous journey.

SALE OF GOODS ACTS

Statutes that codify the rules, many of which have emerged from custom and practice over the years or have long been recognised under COMMON LAW, to regulate the selling of goods to consumers. In particular, they operate to safeguard consumers' rights by imputing certain basic terms as warranties into the sale CONTRACT. Under English law, some of these implied terms are sacrosanct and cannot be excluded, but others may be avoided by agreement between the parties. For example, a seller cannot avoid the implied WARRANTY that he has TITLE to the goods and is empowered to sell them; whereas by agreement with the buyer, he can avoid any LIABILITY for the goods' failure to be of SATISFACTORY QUALITY or fit for any particular purpose. This so-called agreement with the buyer is largely a nonsense, since it is often encapsulated in the microscopic terms and conditions printed on the seller's marketing documents and is forced upon the buyer whether he agrees or not.

SALVAGE
The right to be rewarded for your efforts in rescuing a ship or a ship's cargo from shipwreck. Some jurisdictions recognise this right as an established part of the law, but most leave it to agreement between the parties involved. This can lead to the bizarre result of the captain of a professional salvage vessel negotiating a CONTRACT with the ship's owners as the stricken vessel drifts ever closer to the rocks. Environmental disasters may be avoided, but only if the price is right.

SATISFACTION
To reach agreement with someone over the payment of a debt or settlement of a claim (see ACCORD AND SATISFACTION). A MEMORANDUM OF SATISFACTION is a document that records the settlement of a debt and the release by the creditor of a CHARGE or other SECURITY over the debtor's property. In the UK it is commonly required by a company as proof that a charge has been released, so that the release can be registered against the company's name on the public record at COMPANIES HOUSE.

SATISFACTORY QUALITY
A term introduced in the UK by the Sale and Supply of Goods Act 1994 in substitution for the more well-known MERCHANTABLE QUALITY.

SCHEME OF ARRANGEMENT
An agreement between an individual and his creditors for the payment, usually by instalments, of all or part of his debts by way of SATISFACTION of their claims against him, in order to ward off BANKRUPTCY proceedings. In the UK, if the scheme is approved by the HIGH COURT, it is known as an INDIVIDUAL VOLUNTARY ARRANGEMENT.

SCOTLAND
Scotland has a significantly different system of law

from the rest of the UK. Scottish law has blended concepts from continental Europe, some traditional COMMON LAW principles and its own historical mores to produce a sophisticated, albeit idiosyncratic, form of JURISPRUDENCE. Most well known is the concept of NOT PROVEN, which allows a neutral verdict to be given when a DEFENDANT in a criminal trial cannot be convicted because the prosecution has failed to bring sufficient evidence to prove him guilty. Scotland also has a streamlined system of CONVEYANCE of REAL ESTATE, which allows the buyer and seller to become contractually bound at an early stage (thereby reducing the risk of gazumping).

> *Justice is like a train that's nearly always late.*
> Yevgeny Yevtushenko, 1963

SCRIVENER NOTARY
See NOTARY PUBLIC.

SEAL
A seal is a blob of wax or, if you are really modern, a small red wafer that you must attach to a DEED, next to your signature, to signify that you are serious about entering into binding legal relations. If you do not, the rules say all bets are off and the deed is void. Traditionally, a company will have a mechanical implement to make an indentation of its corporate seal on a deed, against which the directors must sign as evidence that it was properly affixed. Thankfully, the trend of the more far-sighted law-makers is to abolish these archaic rules and they can now be avoided in jurisdictions such as the UK and the USA.

SECURITY
A word with many meanings, both in common usage and in the legal world, depending on the context. Security of TENURE is the right to remain in possession of REAL ESTATE, such as the right to demand the renewal of a LEASE. In the sense of COLLATERAL, it is some form of GUARANTEE that a

S

debtor will pay its debt. In the plural securities are all kinds of investments, such as stocks and shares. (See also SECURITY FOR COSTS.)

SECURITY FOR COSTS

In the UK, unlike in the USA, the successful party in LITIGATION has the right to apply to the court for an order that the loser must pay its legal costs. The fear of the burden of the other side's legal fees, as well as your own, is an effective deterrent against speculative litigation. On the basis of this principle, a DEFENDANT is entitled to know that the PLAINTIFF has sufficient resources to fund this potential LIABILITY. If a defendant can convince a court that there is some doubt about this, or that the plaintiff is a foreigner without significant assets within the court's jurisdiction, the court may grant a STAY OF PROCEEDINGS unless the plaintiff deposits a specified sum with the court as SECURITY for the defendant's costs if the plaintiff fails.

SEED CAPITAL

A rare form of VENTURE CAPITAL, seed capital is an investment in a new venture without any proven worth or track record. This means it carries a high risk for the investor and explains its rarity.

SEISED

Derived from seisin, a noun used in feudal law to mean the legal possession of land, a person who is seised of property is legally in possession of it either as FREEHOLD or under a LEASE.

SEMBLE

An excellent word used with due solemnity by court commentators and compilers of LAW REPORTS when they think the JUDGE has gone completely haywire in his reasoning for a judgement or, more politely, where it appears there is some uncertainty about what the court intended.

SENATE

The upper house of a legislature. The US Senate is one of the houses of CONGRESS and is made up of two elected senators from every state. A BILL of any type may be introduced to the Senate, except for bills relating to finance, which must start in the House of Representatives. The Senate is required to confirm presidential nominations to certain federal appointments, such as the nomination of judges to the SUPREME COURT.

SENIOR DEBT

A loan by a borrower that ranks above another loan, known inevitably as the JUNIOR DEBT. This means the borrower has given a contractual undertaking to pay off the senior debt before the junior debt. Other things being equal, senior debt should be cheaper (that is, at lower interest rates) than the junior debt because the risk is comparatively lower.

SEPARATE PROPERTY

In contrast to COMMUNITY PROPERTY, this is property owned individually and separately by a husband and wife before their marriage. The distinction between community property and separate property is common throughout the world, including the COMMON LAW system of the USA and the CIVIL LAW system of continental Europe, but not in English law which has to resort to EQUITY (with a little help from STATUTE) in this area.

SEPARATION OF POWERS

The constitutional independence of many countries, notably the USA, is built on the principle that power is separated among the three bodies of state: the legislative body, which passes laws; the judiciary, which enforces the law; and the executive, which runs the government. The president cannot sit in CONGRESS; and Congress cannot interfere with the decisions of the courts. This principle is simple and logical. In contrast, the amorphous constitution of the UK is mysterious and haphazard. It is a wonder it works at all, and some people think it does not. First, the powers are not separate. PARLIAMENT has legislative powers to pass laws and judicial powers (where the

House of Lords sits as the final court of APPEAL) to interpret the law. Second, the executive is not independent of the legislature. Members of the government sit and vote in Parliament; indeed, supremacy in the House of Commons (the lower house of Parliament) carries the right to form the government. The reason, of course, for this striking distinction is that constitutional democracy in the UK has emerged and evolved over centuries, whereas the fathers of the US constitution were able to start with a clean sheet.

> *The illegal we do immediately. The*
> *unconstitutional takes a little longer.*
> Henry Kissinger

SEQUESTRATE
To seize property with the authority of the court, particularly where a person has refused to obey a court's order or instructions. A celebrated example arose during the UK miners' strike in the mid-1980s, where the HIGH COURT ordered the sequestration of the assets of the National Union of Mineworkers as a result of the union's refusal to cease secondary picketing.

SERIOUS FRAUD OFFICE
Commonly known by its three-letter acronym, the SFO is the arm of the criminal prosecution service in the UK that deals with serious cases of white-collar crime. It employs a team of experienced accountants and lawyers whose job is to investigate fraud and financial malpractice and to conduct prosecutions where appropriate. The SFO's failure to secure convictions in several high profile cases, such as that of the Maxwell brothers, has led to calls for a reconsideration of its approach.

SERVANT
Betraying its feudal roots and giving a clear signal as to who has the upper hand, UK employment law often refers to employer and employee as master and servant.

SERVICE CONTRACT
A contract of employment between an employer and an employee.

SERVICE MARK
Similar to a TRADE MARK, a service mark is a distinctive name, design or logo under which a trader offers services. It is capable of registration in order to protect it against infringement. In the same way that a trade mark can be registered against a class of goods, a service mark can be registered for specific classes of services.

SERVICE OF PROCESS
Formal delivery of a document, such as a WRIT, to the relevant person. A person may authorise another, such as his lawyer, to accept service of process on his behalf. (See ACKNOWLEDGEMENT OF SERVICE and SUBSTITUTED SERVICE.)

SET DOWN
When a law suit is set down for trial by the court clerk, it means it has been officially posted on the list of actions ready to be heard by the court. The clerk may issue a fixed date or a floating date (that is, put it on the warned list) where it will be heard as soon as earlier cases have finished.

SET OF CHAMBERS
The offices of a group of barristers who work together, not in PARTNERSHIP but sharing the overheads of the office. Together they pay the rent and electricity bills; they also employ a clerk or clerks to act as a go-between in their dealings with solicitors. This gives the clerks, who traditionally take 10% of each BARRISTER's earnings, exceptional power over their masters as they control the lifeblood of work to all of them. Barristers are independent contractors, each working for himself or herself, but like badgers they make their home in a set for collective warmth and security.

SET-OFF
Nothing to do with fireworks, a right of set-off is

exercised where A owes B £100, but B owes A
£20, so A pays B £80 and calls it quits. B may be
unhappy with this, perhaps if he disputes his debt
of £20 to A, but he is in a weak position since A
holds the initiative (and the money) and forces B
to take action to claim whatever he thinks he is
owed. Typically, a bank's loan documents will
expressly prohibit the borrower from exercising
any right of set-off. A bank likes to get all the
money, then argue later about whether it should
give some back.

---

*We have started using lawyers instead of rats for
our laboratory experiments. First, there are more
lawyers than rats. Secondly, some of our
laboratory technicians were becoming
emotionally attached to the rats. And thirdly, in
the final analysis, there are some things a rat
won't do.*
A disgruntled client

SETTLED LAND
REAL ESTATE that is the subject of a TRUST.

SETTLOR
The person who creates a TRUST by settling property (the trust fund) on another (the TRUSTEE).

SEVERAL LIABILITY
A group of people with several LIABILITY are liable
separately as individuals so their creditors must
sue them individually only for the liability
incurred by each of them. A group of people with
JOINT LIABILITY are liable together as a group and
their creditors must sue all of them together for
the liability of the group. A group of people with
joint and several liability are in the soup because
they are liable both together as a group and separately as individuals. This means their creditors
may sue any one of them or all of them for the liability of the whole group. A partner has joint and
several liability for the debts of his PARTNERSHIP.

SEVERANCE

To sever a JOINT TENANCY is to separate joint interests in property, thereby ending the right of survivorship and turning the joint tenancy into a TENANCY IN COMMON.

> *Great cases like hard cases make bad law.*
> Oliver Wendell Holmes, 1904

SEVERANCE PAY

Money paid by an employer to an employee on termination of his or her employment.

SFO

See SERIOUS FRAUD OFFICE.

SHADOW DIRECTOR

A shadow director is a person who exercises some control over the affairs of a company or whose wishes a company invariably follows, even though he or she is not formally appointed as a DIRECTOR. By this definition, the COMPANIES ACTS are able to impose the same duties on shadow directors as they impose on directors. These duties, which carry personal LIABILITY, come into sharp focus when a company is verging on insolvency and a prime candidate for the position of a shadow director is the local bank manager, whose permission is required as a condition for continued banking facilities for every cheque the company writes.

SHARE

A share in a company represents a bundle of ownership rights which the shareholder holds in respect of the company and the other shareholders. These rights are set out in the company's constitution (for a UK company, its MEMORANDUM OF ASSOCIATION and ARTICLES OF ASSOCIATION). The constitution is a multipartite CONTRACT between all the shareholders and its terms can be varied to suit different circumstances with the agreement of all the contractors. Accordingly, there may be different rights, powers or duties attributed to different classes of shares. Some may be devoid of the rights commonly attaching to shares (for example, without any right to vote or share in dividends) so that they no longer look like shares. Others may have weighted voting rights which give effective control over the company. As George Orwell might have said, all shares are equal but some are more equal than others.

SILK
An informal term for a QUEEN'S COUNSEL.

SINE DIE
A commonly used and usually mispronounced Latin phrase meaning "without specifying a day". A court hearing may be adjourned *sine die*, meaning adjourned to some date in the future as yet unspecified.

SLANDER
See DEFAMATION.

SOLICITOR
A solicitor is one type of English legal professional, the other being a BARRISTER; the distinction is famously difficult to explain. First, it is wrong to think that solicitors make up half of the legal profession because there are many, many more of them than barristers. Second, it is wrong to assume that the barrister does all the court work, as many solicitors spend their careers in court (even on their feet, as advocates, although typically not in the higher courts). Third, as the distinction between the two becomes increasingly blurred, it is possible to find barristers employed by solicitors' firms (although they may have to recant their heresy, and renounce the bar, before being allowed into PARTNERSHIP with solicitors).

It is perhaps more helpful to record a few certainties. Barristers work alone as independent contractors, although they band together in a SET OF CHAMBERS for administrative convenience. Solicitors frequently work in partnerships, with the big firms having hundreds of partners. Barristers usually specialise, even if only in advocacy, whereas many solicitors' firms offer a full legal service including CONVEYANCE, LITIGATION, TRUST, MERGERS AND ACQUISITIONS, family and general commercial work. Barristers do, solicitors do not, wear wigs. Barristers belong to and are governed by the INNS OF COURT. Solicitors are governed by the LAW SOCIETY. In summary, using a medical analogy, solicitors can be seen as the general practitioners (notwithstanding that many of them do specialise) and barristers are the consultants or specialists.

Lawyers load men with intolerable burdens, and will not put a single finger to the load.
The Bible, *St Luke*

SOLICITOR-GENERAL
A member of PARLIAMENT and one of the LAW OFFICERS, the solicitor-general acts as deputy to the ATTORNEY-GENERAL. Merely to confuse everyone, he is invariably a BARRISTER. The solicitor-general for SCOTLAND is deputy to the LORD ADVOCATE.

SOLUS AGREEMENT
An agreement where one party agrees to acquire all of its supplies, such as petrol or beer, from the other party. In theory agreements of this type are anti-competitive since they restrict the freedom of the purchaser from shopping around for better prices or quality, and they fall within the scope of the European competition rules of the TREATY OF ROME and the ANTI-TRUST legislation of the USA. However, vested interests and compelling economic arguments have succeeded in overcoming this LEGISLATION to a large degree. Hamburger franchises and petrol stations around the world remain bound by solus agreements.

SPECIAL RESOLUTION
A resolution of the MEMBERS of a UK company, which either by law or by the company's ARTICLES OF ASSOCIATION must be passed by at least 75% of

those voting. Such resolutions relate to the most important issues facing a company, such as changing its constitution or entering into a WINDING UP. (In contrast, see ORDINARY RESOLUTION.)

SPECIALITY CONTRACT
A CONTRACT made under SEAL.

SPECIFIC PERFORMANCE
An order of a court to the effect that one party to a CONTRACT must perform its contractual obligations to the other party. A litigant is often faced with the choice of seeking specific performance or DAMAGES where it suffers a breach of contract.

SSAP
See STATEMENTS OF STANDARD ACCOUNTING PRACTICE.

STAKEHOLDER
Someone who holds money on behalf of the parties to a CONTRACT, with instructions to hand it over to one of them on the happening of a certain event. On signing a contract for the acquisition of REAL ESTATE, the purchaser may pay a deposit to a stakeholder with instructions that it should only be handed to the seller on COMPLETION of the contract. If the seller fails to complete the contract, the stakeholder is instructed to return the deposit to the purchaser. If the stakeholder earns any interest on the money while it is in his possession, he should hand it over with the principal sum.

STAMP DUTY
A tax on legal documents that is about as modern and sophisticated as a tax that used to exist in England, levied on the number of windows in a house. However, it is retained by successive governments because it is an easy and efficient way of raising revenue. In the UK its main application is on documents for the CONVEYANCE of land and for the transfer of shares. In both cases it is levied AD VALOREM to the value of the asset transferred and is enforced by the simple rule that a purchaser cannot rely on the purchase CONTRACT in a UK court

S

unless it has been duly stamped. There have been and still are numerous schemes to avoid paying stamp duty, but many of them are no more sophisticated than the tax itself and depend on the parties leaving the UK for a day to have a satisfying lunch in France or the Channel Islands, signing their contracts and leaving them there outside the jurisdiction of the UK courts. Faced with the introduction of a paperless procedure for SHARE transactions (no paper to stamp, no stamp duty), the UK government has brought in stamp duty reserve tax, which taxes the transaction rather than the document.

STATEMENT OF CLAIM
The details of a PLAINTIFF's claim against a DEFENDANT as set out in a WRIT or a document ancillary to the writ.

STATEMENTS OF STANDARD ACCOUNTING PRACTICE
A set of rules, commonly known by the acronym SSAP, devised by accountants on how to draw up a UK company's accounts (FINANCIAL STATEMENTS). The rules started with the praiseworthy goal of providing consistency in corporate accounting, but as far as ordinary people are concerned they have become lost in a morass of detail and complexity. The rules are continuously under review and are periodically supplemented by new ones. Some of them follow international precedent but others do not. In the USA and Europe equivalent circumstances can have quite different treatment.

STATUTE
A written law brought into being by a country's law-making machinery as LEGISLATION. In the UK statutes are passed by PARLIAMENT as acts of Parliament. In the USA bills are passed by CONGRESS as acts.

STATUTE-BARRED
The extinguishment or lapse of a right because it has not been enforced within the time limit set down in the STATUTE of limitations (see LIMITATION PERIOD).

STAY OF PROCEEDINGS

An order by a court that an action will be stopped or halted until a specified condition has been fulfilled. For example, an action may be stayed unless a PLAINTIFF deposits money in response to a DEFENDANT's successful application for SECURITY FOR COSTS.

STIPENDIARY MAGISTRATE

A magistrate with legal qualifications in full-time paid employment, as opposed to an unpaid JUSTICE OF THE PEACE.

> *I consider myself a passionate man, but, of course, a lawyer first.*
> Charles Barsotti

STOCK

In investment terms, stock is often used as a generic term for all kinds of shares and securities issued by a company. In legal terms, stock can and should be distinguished from shares. Shares are the rights granted to the owners of a company through which they derive the benefits of ownership (for example, by receiving dividends) and exercise some level of control (for example, by voting at a GENERAL MEETING). All of these rights can be varied: some shares have no right to dividends, others carry no voting powers. Nevertheless, the concept of shares envisages these fundamental rights of corporate ownership. Stock, on the other hand, can be seen as something different from ownership, although at times the rights and powers attaching to stock can be indistinguishable from those attaching to shares. Stock, in its true sense, is the capitalisation of a loan to a company or to a government. As with all loans, it is intended to be repaid. Stock should be REDEEMABLE whereas ordinary shares should not. Stock in all its disguises should be seen as a loan; shares should be seen as ownership. (See DEBENTURE.)

SUBCONTRACT

A CONTRACT between the main contractor of a project and a third-party supplier of goods or services, for whom the main contractor becomes responsible (to the ultimate customer) by virtue of the terms of the main contract. You enter into a contract with a builder to renovate your house. This contract includes everything, including plumbing, electrics and decorating, even though the builder himself only does structural construction work. For the plumbing, electrics and decorating, he enters into subcontracts with specialist plumbers, electricians and decorators. You are not concerned with (or even aware of) the terms of these subcontracts. All the terms that concern you are set out in the main contract. The builder (as the main contractor) chooses which parts he will perform himself and which he will subcontract. He remains liable to you, however, for the delivery of the whole project.

SUBJECT TO CONTRACT

Not legally binding. An agreement that is not intended to be binding on the parties unless and until it is confirmed in a written CONTRACT signed by them. If you are embarking on negotiations that you hope will eventually result in a binding contract, but want to see the final picture before agreeing to be bound, you should make clear from the outset that your negotiations are subject to contract. By convention you do this by writing these words on the first written communication you send to the other side. If you do not, you might unwittingly bind yourself to something without intending to do so. This should not be confused with WITHOUT PREJUDICE.

SUB JUDICE

Latin for "under adjudication". A case that is *sub judice* is in the course of the trial process and no judgement has yet been reached. The inference is that unrestricted media comment might prejudice its outcome, so press reporting or other public pronouncements on it are restricted. Failure to abide by this constitutes a CONTEMPT OF COURT.

SUBORDINATION

The ranking of a right below another right. If a loan to a borrower is subordinated to another loan, the other loan has to be repaid first or else the borrower will be in breach of CONTRACT to the other lender.

SUBPOENA

A court order requiring you to appear before a court as a witness and answer questions under OATH.

> *We have a criminal jury system which is superior to any in the world; and its efficiency is only marred by the difficulty of finding twelve men every day who don't know anything and can't read.*
> Mark Twain

SUBROGATION

A vital principle for the insurance world. Subrogation entitles someone to stand in the shoes of someone else and pursue whatever legal claim that person may have against a third party. An insurance CONTRACT on your house will provide cover if a truck driver deposits his vehicle in the front of your home. Your insurer will reimburse you for the cost of the repairs, but this is not necessarily the end of the story. Under the principle of subrogation, the insurer will be entitled to sue the truck driver in your name for the recovery of DAMAGES caused by his wayward driving.

SUBSCRIBER

Someone who applies for shares in a new company that is about to be formed. Subscriber shares are the first shares issued when a company is incorporated.

SUBSTITUTED SERVICE

Nothing to do with swapping players late in the second half, substituted service is SERVICE OF PROCESS by some means other than the usual method.

S

For example, where a DEFENDANT has disappeared, a court may allow substituted service by post to his last known address or by advertising in designated newspapers.

SUCCESSION
The law of succession determines how someone acquires TITLE to property when the owner dies. If the owner has left a WILL, title will be transferred by his executors following the grant of PROBATE. If there is no will, the INTESTATE rules will apply. If you are the monarch, the law of succession will also work out who becomes the next king or queen.

SUFFERANCE
Acquiescence; putting up with something, possibly reluctantly, and being bound to recognise it by law. If, as a landlord, you allow your tenant to stay in occupation (HOLDING OVER) after the expiry of the LEASE, the tenant may claim (and the law may recognise) a tenancy at sufferance which you cannot deny.

SUI GENERIS
Latin for "of its own kind". A legal right that exists as a class of its own, rather than merely being recognised as an extension of another right. The law of NEGLIGENCE has emerged as a right *sui generis*, not just an adjunct to another TORT.

SUMMARY JUDGEMENT
An application to a court by one party to ask the court to find for him immediately, without further ado in the LITIGATION process, on the ground that the other side has no viable argument to resist it. A PLAINTIFF may ask for summary judgement on the ground that the DEFENDANT has no viable defence. A defendant may ask for the action against him to be struck out on summary judgement on the ground that the plaintiff has failed to establish a viable case. If you are lucky, it is a quick solution to an otherwise painful process.

SUMMING UP

The final remarks made by a JUDGE to a JURY at the end of a trial, summarising the main arguments and points of evidence, before the jury retires to consider its verdict. The summing up has to be done with care. The judge may leave himself open to an APPEAL if he appears to be partisan or otherwise misdirects the jury.

SUMMONS

A WRIT is the first step in LITIGATION in the HIGH COURT; a summons is the equivalent in the COUNTY COURT.

SUPREME COURT

The Supreme Court of Judicature is the highest court in England and Wales and comprises the HIGH COURT and the Court of APPEAL. In the USA the Supreme Court of Justice is the final court of appeal in the federal court system with celebrated jurists appointed as its judges by the president.

Convicted criminal: *As God is my judge, I am innocent.*
Judge Birkett: *He isn't, I am and you're not.*

SURVIVORSHIP

The right of survivorship applies only to a JOINT TENANCY. If two or more people own property as joint tenants (as opposed to tenants in common) and one of them dies, the deceased person's interest in the property is automatically transferred to the surviving owner or owners, not the deceased's heirs.

SWEAT EQUITY

In a VENTURE CAPITAL transaction, sweat equity is that part of the management's investment attributed to their hard work and dedication to the business and accordingly awarded to them without a corresponding cash investment. For a good example of how this is used as an incentive for future performance, see RATCHET.

SYLLABUS

In a US LAW REPORT the syllabus is the summary of the case which appears at the beginning.

SYNDICATION

A syndicated loan or investment in a company is one shared by several participants. A bank or financial institution will usually take the lead (known obscurely as the lead bank) in assessing the investment and inviting other investors to participate. Syndication occurs primarily where the investment is too large for a single investor to carry happily on its books, but it may also be because it is too risky and a bank feels nervous being out there all on its own.

TABLE A
A standard form of ARTICLES OF ASSOCIATION appended to the COMPANIES ACTS. These articles may be adopted by a company, with or without amendment, by simple reference in its own articles of association.

TAKEOVER PANEL
An official body situated in London that regulates MERGERS AND ACQUISITIONS of companies listed on the London Stock Exchange. Its role is particularly pertinent in hostile takeovers, where one side is likely to complain about the conduct of the other side merely as a strategic ploy. The panel acts as a referee to ensure a good, clean fight with no holding or head-butting.

TARGET COMPANY
The object of the takeover in a corporate acquisition.

TAXING MASTER
See MASTER.

TECHNOLOGY TRANSFER
A US term for a CONTRACT in the form of a LICENCE (or, in the USA, a license) whereby one party allows another to use its KNOW-HOW or other technological process in return for a ROYALTY or other payment.

TENANCY IN COMMON
In contrast to a JOINT TENANCY, a tenancy in common is where two or more people hold separate interests in the same property. Each of them may deal with his or her share as they please, without the involvement of the others. If one dies the interest passes to the deceased's estate, not to the other tenants in common.

TENDER
An OFFER to enter into a CONTRACT. If you invite tenders for a project, you are asking potential contractors to make an offer to carry out the work on

stated terms. You can then compare the competing bids and accept the one that seems most attractive. Notification of your acceptance constitutes formation of the contract. A sale of property by sealed tender invites potential purchasers to submit sealed bids, all of which will be opened on a specified date, with the implication that the seller will sell to the highest bidder.

TENURE

Your right, and possibly the limited extent of your right, to hold REAL ESTATE. Security of tenure means you have a continuing right, such as the right to call for a renewal of a LEASE on its expiry.

TERMINATION CLAUSE

A term of a CONTRACT that sets out how and when a party may bring the contract to an end before its expected expiry date. A failure by the other party to perform its obligations (possibly after a CURE PERIOD), or the insolvency or a change in the circumstances of the other party are common examples. A well-drafted contract will also include the agreed consequences of termination, such as who keeps what or who pays whom.

TESTATOR

A man who makes a WILL.

TESTATRIX

A woman who makes a WILL.

TESTIMONIUM CLAUSE

The words used at the end of a legal document, such as a CONTRACT or WILL, where the parties put their signatures. The clause can be pompous (in witness whereof I have hereunto set my hand and seal the day first above written) or straightforward (signed by the duly authorised representatives of the parties).

TIME IMMEMORIAL

The full extent of legal memory, which is everything after 1189 (although we have forgotten why this year was important). If something has occurred since time immemorial, it has been going on so long no one can remember when it started.

TIME OF THE ESSENCE

A tricky, and somewhat arbitrary, rule of CONTRACT law. In general terms, the law believes that there should always be some leeway in enforcing time periods in contracts. If your garage promises to repair your car within four days and it takes five days, the law is unlikely to get too excited. If you expect your consignment of widgets to be delivered on September 12th but it is a week late, you probably do not have any claim. The situation would be different if there was an unreasonable delay, say, weeks for your car or months for your beans, but generally there is some leeway. If, however, you write in the contract the magic words "time is of the essence of the contract" everything changes. All of a sudden time is deemed to be vital. This little phrase is supposed to signal the parties' intention to be held to a strict timetable. One day late, and you are liable.

I don't want a lawyer to tell me what I cannot do; I hire him to tell me how to do what I want to do.
J. Pierpont Morgan

TIME SUMMONS

An application to a court asking for more time to do something required to be done in the LITIGATION process, such as filing a defence or another stage in the PLEADINGS.

TIPSTAFF

A court official who is responsible for enforcing good order in court and, on the JUDGE's instructions, arresting someone who is in CONTEMPT OF COURT.

TITLE

The right of ownership of property, either goods

or real estate. To have good title to something
means that you are the uncontested owner, without any limit or ENCUMBRANCE on your right of ownership. QUALIFIED TITLE means there is some defect
in your claim to ownership.

TOLL
In US legal parlance, to toll a law is to suspend it
temporarily.

TORT
Literally a "wrong", a tort is a spongy COMMON LAW
concept that describes various reasons why one
person may be liable to another. Unlike CONTRACT
law, where the existence of LIABILITY depends on
the existence of a binding agreement between the
parties, a tort can exist without any contract or
even contact between the parties. The law of tort
is founded on the existence of a duty of care
between one person and another. For example,
motorists have a duty to all road users to drive
with care. Journalists have a duty not to libel their
subjects. Failure to live up to these duties gives
rise to a tort: in the respective examples, the torts
of NEGLIGENCE and LIBEL. If a tort occurs, the victim
has a right of action for damages against the perpetrator (the tortfeasor). At common law, an
action (a suit or proceedings) can be founded
only in contract or in tort.

TRACING
You undertake a tracing action to recover money
wrongfully taken from you and either passed
through several hands or converted into other
property. The action may be directed against
innocent third parties, such as banks, which may
be holding the funds without any knowledge of
the wrongdoing. Alternatively, it may seek to
establish an OVERREACHING interest in an asset pur-
chased with misappropriated funds or in the proceeds of the sale of a misappropriated asset.

TRADE MARK
Where someone carries on business under a

name, design or logo with a distinctive style that is peculiar to and identifies his business or products, he can claim this as his trade mark. Establishing a trade mark depends on overcoming competing claims of other traders, so you have to show that your mark is distinctive and is identified with your business by virtue of your use of it. Although a trade mark can exist and be defended without any formal registration, there are trade mark registries in all the world's major trading countries (linked by international treaties), which provide for protection through a formal registration process. Registration is granted in different classes of goods and the applicant will be allowed to protect his mark only in a class where he can demonstrate sufficient use of the mark with the goods in that class. A trade mark owner in one class cannot complain about an infringement of his mark by someone trading in another class, although he may have a claim as a PASSING OFF action.

TRANSCRIPT
A verbatim record of everything said in the course of a trial, noted by a court official and made available to the participants.

TREASURE TROVE
The discovery of long-hidden treasure. If you find some treasure in the UK (on your way to work or wherever), you are obliged to notify your local CORONER who, in between inquests into violent or otherwise untimely deaths, will hold an INQUEST into treasure trove. There are some marvellous distinctions between treasure that has been simply lost as opposed to deliberately hidden, but the upshot is that if it is decided that it has been deliberately hidden, it is treasure trove and belongs to the Crown (that is, the state) as BONA VACANTIA. However, even if it is and you have to hand it over, there is usually a reward.

TREATY OF ROME
A treaty signed by the original founding members to create the European Economic Community

(EEC) in 1957. It has been signed by all subsequent joining states and still forms the basis of the economic and political relations between members of the European Union (EU). Its provisions have been supplemented over time; for example, by the Maastricht treaty, which introduced a range of social as well as economic objectives. The most frequently quoted provisions of the Treaty of Rome are Articles 85 and 86, which are the foundation of ANTI-TRUST LEGISLATION in the EU.

TRESPASS

A TORT, trespass is interfering with someone's property rights by going on to his land without permission, or interfering with his goods, or interfering with his person.

TRUST

Trust law conjures up visions of Dickensian legal concepts, argued over for years in cases such as *Jarndyce v Jarndyce*, but in fact the trust concept has proved infinitely durable and flexible. Trust law forms the basis of charities, investment vehicles (unit trusts), pension schemes, project financing arrangements and many other ingenious schemes designed to hold funds for specified purposes. The essence of a trust is that one person (the TRUSTEE) holds property (the trust fund) on behalf of and for the benefit of another (the BENEFICIARY). Trust law lays down rules as to how the trustee must act and what powers he, she or it may exercise over the trust fund. It also makes the trustee personally liable if the property is misappropriated, so the job should not be taken on lightly.

Probably the most common example of a trust is the administration of a deceased person's ESTATE. The executors under the WILL are trustees of the estate and they become the legal owners of the deceased's assets. They hold these assets in trust for the beneficiaries (those who are to benefit from them) and must account to the beneficiaries for the trust fund. Thus there is a distinction between the legal interest (held by the trustees) and the beneficial interest (held by the beneficiaries). This division of interests is the foundation of trust law. A bare trust, as opposed to a DISCRETIONARY TRUST, gives no discretion to the trustee in the administration of the trust fund. He, she or it must account to the beneficiaries for the trust fund without further ado. They cannot choose to favour one beneficiary over another or decide to invest the trust fund for future distribution. The beneficiary has an established and immediate right to call for the relevant share of the trust fund. The trustee must honour it; a court must enforce it.

Judge: *I have listened to you, Mr Smith, but I am none the wiser.*
F.E. Smith: *Possibly not, m'Lud, but you are much better informed.*

TRUSTEE
A person holding property subject to a TRUST.

TRUSTEE IN BANKRUPTCY
See BANKRUPTCY.

TUPE

Pronounced "tew-pee", this is an acronym for the Transfer of Undertakings (Protection of Employment) Regulations 1981. The only thing the legal fraternity can agree about TUPE is that it is badly drafted. Some people maintain total enmity to it, claiming it represents a major change to social law by the back door (it was introduced by parliamentary regulations, rather than a fully constituted STATUTE). Others say it is a cornerstone of employment rights, as endorsed by continued developments in European law. So what is the issue? In substance, TUPE provides an automatic mechanism to transfer employees' rights from one employer to another when the business in which they work is sold (transferred). Thus they cannot be forced to accept a new CONTRACT on less favourable terms than their existing one and their accrued employment rights (such as length of service for REDUN-

DANCY purposes) may be enforced against the new employer. Problems abound over the interpretation of almost every word in TUPE: what constitutes an undertaking, when has there been a transfer and so on. One point to remember is that TUPE is relevant only to a transfer of a business (that is, an UNDERTAKING), not the transfer of shares in a company. In the case of a SHARE acquisition, the purchaser acquires the company with all its assets and liabilities, warts and all, including the employees and the contractual burden of their accrued employment rights. There is no need for any mechanism to provide for their transfer.

TURNKEY CONTRACT

A form of CONTRACT in the construction industry where the contractor undertakes to build and equip a site ready for an industrial process to commence. The project may be a timber mill or an oil refinery or whatever. The contractor delivers a working facility to the client, who on completion merely has to turn the key in the door and walk into a fully operational site.

U

UBERRIMAE FIDEI

Latin for "of the utmost good faith". The law recognises that certain relationships, such as that of partners in a PARTNERSHIP, require the participants to act towards each other with a higher duty of care than in normal, arm's-length relationships. This requires them to be doubly virtuous in their dealings with each other; they should have no secrets, no hidden agendas and no competing interests.

ULTRA VIRES

To act outside the scope of the powers you have authority to exercise. In other words, the opposite of INTRA VIRES.

UNCONDITIONAL

A slice of MERGERS AND ACQUISITIONS jargon. When a takeover offer for a TARGET COMPANY is said to go unconditional, it has been accepted by a majority of the company's shareholders and the conditions attached to the offer no longer apply. In short, it is a euphemism for "we've won; we've acquired the company; make way for the triumphal march".

UNDERLEASE

A sublease; a LEASE of REAL ESTATE by a tenant whose interest derives from a lease from his landlord.

UNDERTAKING

It can mean either a commitment or promise given in a CONTRACT, or a business or trade carried on for commercial profit. For the rules of employment law that apply to the transfer of an undertaking in the UK, see TUPE.

UNDERWRITE

To underwrite an issue of shares is to promise to subscribe for and purchase any shares not taken up by the primary subscribers. Before a company embarks on a FLOTATION or other offering of shares to the public, it will usually enter into an underwriting agreement with a merchant (investment) bank, which, for a large fee, will agree to subscribe for any shares not taken up in the public offer. This enables the company to be confident that the capital-raising project will be successful; whatever happens, all the offered shares will be sold.

UNDUE INFLUENCE

Pressure exerted on someone to cause them to do something they would not otherwise do. It can be a ground for challenging a WILL or to avoid a CONTRACT, but it is successful only in exceptional circumstances where the court considers that the individual concerned (almost seen as the victim) was particularly vulnerable. A classic example is when an old person changes their will in favour of their housekeeper, thereby disinheriting a family line of umpteen generations; the family will claim that the housekeeper has been manipulative whereas the truth may be that the housekeeper was genuinely closer to the deceased than his or her relatives.

If you study the history and records of the world, you must admit that the source of justice was the fear of injustice.
Horace, 35 BC

UNINCORPORATED ASSOCIATION

An organisation, such as a club or a PARTNERSHIP, that is not incorporated as a company.

UNLIMITED COMPANY

A company, incorporated with the usual formalities, whose shareholders do not have any limit on their LIABILITY to support it. If the company incurs losses, the shareholders must continue to contribute funds to it in order to satisfy the losses.

VACANT POSSESSION

Where REAL ESTATE is sold with vacant possession, it means the vendor is giving a WARRANTY to the purchaser that he will be able to occupy it immediately on completion of the sale. If immediate occupation is denied for some reason, the vendor may be liable to pay DAMAGES or the purchaser may be able to claim RESCISSION of the sale.

VENTURE CAPITAL

This is the sharp end of the capitalist system. Venture capital is EQUITY CAPITAL provided to a PRIVATE COMPANY to get its business started or to help it expand. This means it is a risky investment and usually it comes from specialist finance houses (venture capitalists) which claim expertise in spotting good horses in a novices' handicap. They often offer management expertise to their chosen runners and get closely involved with their businesses. At first the venture capitalists maintain a common agenda with the company's management, but inevitably this diverges as the venture capitalists' prime concern is to find a way to realise their investment (their exit) over the medium term in order to reinvest their funds elsewhere. Outside fast-growing new technologies, such as health care and information technology, venture capital is largely directed towards proven businesses rather than start-up ventures (see the distinction between SEED CAPITAL and DEVELOPMENT CAPITAL). It frequently figures in the financial backing for the acquisition of a business by its managers from its owners (see MANAGEMENT BUY-OUT).

VEXATIOUS

Vexatious LITIGATION is a legal claim without foundation that is pursued by a PLAINTIFF out of malice for the DEFENDANT.

VICARIOUS

Where an employee commits a TORT in the course of his employment, his employer may be liable to compensate a third party who has suffered damage. This indirect LIABILITY is called vicarious liability. It is particularly useful for finding a pocket deep enough to pay substantial DAMAGES. If a labourer, engaged to mend the garden fence, negligently knocks down your house, he may not have sufficient wealth to meet the compensation. His employer, however, is a better prospect, not least because he should have insurance to cover such eventualities. Vicarious liability is the mechanism used by the law to lay responsibility at the feet of the employer. Problems arise, inevitably, where the employee is acting outside the scope of his employment. In our example, if the labourer wilfully deserts his fence-mending duties and takes a joy-ride in a bulldozer from a neighbouring building site, thereby knocking down your house, it would be unreasonable to hold his employer liable. Vicarious liability applies only where an employee is acting in the course of his employment.

Law is a bottomless pit.
Dr Arbuthnot, 1712

VOID
See NULL AND VOID.

VOLENTI NON FIT INJURIA
Latin for "it is not a wrong if the person consents". You cannot sue someone for an injury (a TORT) if you voluntarily agreed to accept the risk of suffering it. If you decide it is a good idea to climb into a boxing ring for 15 rounds with the world champion, and he breaks your nose, the law expects you not to complain about it. This example is fairly straightforward, but there are areas of argument. If the world champ breaks your nose with a head-butt, which is against the rules, you may have an action against him on the ground that you consented to risk injury only provided that the fight was conducted within the rules. He would counter this, no doubt, by claiming that a head-butt is reasonably foreseeable and fairly common (albeit illegal) in a boxing match, and therefore

you should be deemed to have accepted the risk of it. In conclusion, it is advisable to consult your lawyer before embarking on dangerous sports.

If there were not bad people, there would be no good lawyers.
Charles Dickens, *The Old Curiosity Shop*

WAIVER

Voluntarily giving up a right or releasing someone from performing an obligation due to you. If you waive a condition to a CONTRACT, you consent to the non-performance of the condition and allow the contract to proceed as if the condition had been fulfilled.

WARD OF COURT

A MINOR who is declared to be under the protection of a court in his or her own interest and whose affairs are managed by (or only with the approval of) the court. By assuming a wardship, the court takes on the rights and responsibilities of the ward's parents.

WARRANT

An official document issued by a court giving someone power to do something; for example, a warrant for the arrest of someone or a search warrant.

WARRANTY

In a CONTRACT a condition is a primary provision of the contract. If there is a breach of a condition, the injured party may have the right of RESCISSION to declare the contract NULL AND VOID. A warranty is a secondary provision of a contract. If there is a breach of a warranty, the injured party is able to claim DAMAGES only for the loss suffered, not rescission. As a refinement on this, where goods are sold with a warranty from the supplier, the warranty is a contractual promise that the supplier will repair or replace the goods free of charge if they fail to perform as intended during the warranty period. The customer has to rely on this promise of replacement, rather than demanding rescission of the contract. In many jurisdictions this restricted remedy (under COMMON LAW rules) has been extended by LEGISLATION to enhance the rights of consumers and often grants an overriding right to demand rescission for a serious breach of warranty.

WHITE BOOK
The book of procedural rules of the HIGH COURT.

WILFUL NEGLECT
Intentionally not doing something that you have a duty to do, thereby giving rise to a TORT or a breach of CONTRACT. Wilful neglect is something more than neglect (or NEGLIGENCE) and leaves the perpetrator open to PUNITIVE DAMAGES.

WILL
Your last will and testament is your formal instruction to your executors as to what to do with your property after your death. For the most part, a valid will must be written and signed by the TESTATOR in the presence of at least two witnesses. There are some hideously complicated rules about the witnesses signing in the presence of the testator, but not necessarily in each other's presence, or something like that. It is probably best if everyone signs together. The one rule that everyone knows about the witnesses is that they cannot receive anything under the will, so asking someone to witness your will is a good way of putting an end to that person's misplaced expectations. Confirmation that the will is valid is given by the court on the grant of PROBATE, which in turn serves as authority for the executors to act on behalf of the deceased's ESTATE. The law is really interested in wills only when something goes wrong or some dispossessed malcontent challenges its validity; for example, by suggesting that the testator was insane at the time or was subject to UNDUE INFLUENCE. Then everyone, except the leading actor in the saga, goes off to court for a legal action that lasts years and devours all the assets of the deceased's estate solely for the benefit of the lawyers.

WINDING UP
See LIQUIDATION.

WITH COSTS
In the English courts, if a PLAINTIFF is awarded a

judgement with costs the court has decided that (in addition to the main award) he is entitled to recover his legal costs from the DEFENDANT. Similarly, if the defendant successfully defends the action, he is usually entitled to have his legal costs paid by the plaintiff. If not agreed between the parties, the amount of costs payable will be assessed by a TAXING MASTER and will usually be less than the sum actually incurred. In the US system, save for exceptional circumstances, it is rare for either party to be required to pay the costs of the other.

WITHOUT PREJUDICE

Do not hold it against me. If you are trying to negotiate a settlement to a dispute, either before or after it dissolves into LITIGATION, you can put forward a proposal under the without prejudice banner so that, if negotiations fail, the other side cannot produce your proposal in court as evidence of your admission of LIABILITY. This concept can produce bizarre play in the litigation game. It is not uncommon for a litigation lawyer to write two letters to the other side, sent in the same envelope. The first (sent without any qualification and known as the OPEN letter) refutes every argument put forward by them and accuses them of every dastardly trick imaginable; the second (sent without prejudice) meekly offers some payment by way of settlement. There are several advantages to this tactic. The open letter is intended to soften up the other side to make them appreciate the strength of your case and the tenacity of your defence. In contrast, the without prejudice offer is supposed to look attractive. Further, if the offer is rejected, the only letter to go before court (if it comes to that) is the open letter and thus you have maintained, in the eyes of the court, your consistent and steadfast opposition to the other side's allegations. A neat trick not to be confused with SUBJECT TO CONTRACT.

WRIT

The first step in LITIGATION, a writ is a written

notice that the issuer (the PLAINTIFF) intends to pursue court proceedings against the person to whom it is delivered (the DEFENDANT). It must be in a prescribed form, acknowledged and stamped by the court, and must give sufficient details of the wrong complained of. These details are set out in a STATEMENT OF CLAIM. If the defendant wishes to contest the action, he must file an ACKNOWLEDGEMENT OF SERVICE at the court within a prescribed time limit.

When I grow up, I want to be an honest lawyer so things like that can't happen.
The young Richard Nixon on Teapot Dome scandal

ZIPPER CLAUSE

US jargon for a provision in a CONTRACT that seeks to restrict the negotiation or renegotiation of an issue during the term of the contract. Typically, an employment contract might provide that the remuneration provisions can be reviewed with effect only from a specified date each year. Once it has been resolved, the issue is zipped up until next year.

Part 3
APPENDIXES

1 Glossary of Latin terms

A fortiori	for a compelling reason
Ad valorem	to the value of
Affidavit	he has said it (a sworn statement)
Bona vacantia	vacant goods; goods without an owner
Caveat emptor	buyer beware
De minimis non curat lex	the law is not concerned with trivial matters
Eiusdem generis	of the same kind
Ex gratia	as a favour; without liability
Ex parte	on behalf of one party
Fieri facias	make it happen
Functus officio	having shot one's bolt; spent
Habeas corpus	let him have his body back
Habendum	the part of a conveyance of real estate that describes how the property is to be transferred to the transferee
Ignorantia legis non excusat	ignorance of the law is not an excuse
In flagrante delicto	in the act of committing a crime
In personam	in respect of the person; personalty
In re	in the matter of
In rem	in respect of the thing; realty
Inter alia	among other things
Inter partes	between the parties
Inter vivos	between living people
Intra vires	within the permitted powers
Ipso facto	by the very fact itself
Jurat	the prescribed form of words at the end of an affidavit that show when and where it was sworn

Lex	law
Lex fori	the law of the place where the case is being heard
Lex loci	the law of the place where the act was done
Locus standi	official standing; recognition
Mala in se	wrongs in themselves
Mala prohibita	forbidden wrongs
Mandamus	we command
Mens rea	guilty mind
Mutatis mutandis	change and change about
Nemine contradicente (nem. con.)	with no-one speaking against
Nemo dat quod non habet (nemo dat)	no one can give what he does not have
Nolle prosequi	do not pursue
Non est factum	it is not his act (he did not mean to do it)
Noscitur a sociis	let him be known by the society he keeps
Obiter dicta	incidental comments
Pari passu	of equal power
Prima facie	on the face of it
Quantum meruit	as much as he deserves
Ratio decidendi	the reason for deciding
Regina	the queen
Res ipsa loquitur	it speaks for itself
Res judicata	something on which judgement has already been given
Rex	the king
Sine die	without specifying a day
Sub judice	under adjudication
Sui generis	of its own kind

Uberrimae fidei	of the utmost good faith
Ultra vires	outside the permitted powers
Volenti non fit injuria	it is not a wrong if the person consents

2 Lawyer numbers

	No. of lawyers	Lawyers per 100,000 pop.
Austria	3,086	39
Baltic states	940	12
Belgium	3,000	30
Bulgaria	7,000	79
Canada	68,428	231
China	70,000	6
Cyprus	1,000	142
Czech Rep	2,641	26
Denmark	3,776	73
England & Wales	71,721[a]	120
Finland	1,202	24
France	31,700	56
Germany	67,562	86
Gibraltar	109	363
Greece	23,000	230
Guernsey	47	78
Hong Kong	3,376	56
Hungary	940	9
Iceland	386	148
India	100,000	11
Indonesia	1,200	1
Ireland	4,827[b]	138
Italy	60,000	100
Japan	15,000	12
Jersey	129	152
Liechtenstein	49	163
Luxembourg	261	65
Malaysia	4,000	21
Malta	310	86
Monaco	16	53
Myanmar	1,600	4
Netherlands	7,929	53
Northern Ireland	1,855[c]	116
Norway	3,411	85
Philippines	100,000[d]	152
Poland	24,000	62
Portugal	8,281	84
Russia	18,644	13
Scotland	9,846[e]	197
Singapore	3,000	100

	No. of lawyers	Lawyers per 100,000 pop.
South Korea	3,000	7
Spain	58,000	148
Sweden	3,175	37
Switzerland	5,167	76
Taiwan	3,000	15
Thailand	25,000	43
Turkey	30,319	50
Ukraine	6,000	12
United States	946,499	363

a 63,628 solicitors, 8,093 barristers.   b 3,873 solicitors, 955 barristers.
c 1,492 solicitors, 362 barristers.   d Only 30% practise.   e 352 advocates.

Sources: The European Legal 500 1996 edition; *The Asia Pacific Legal 500* 1996/97 edition; American Bar Association; Canadian Bar Association.

3 Largest law firms

UK

	No. of lawyers	City	Telephone
Clifford Chance	1,459	London	+44 171 600 1000
Eversheds	1,028	London	+44 171 919 4500
Linklaters & Paines	922	London	+44 171 606 7080
Freshfields	819	London	+44 171 936 4000
Lovell White Durrant	739	London	+44 171 236 0066
Allen & Overy	704	London	+44 171 330 3000
Simmons & Simmons	615	London	+44 171 628 2020
Slaughter & May	577	London	+44 171 600 1200
Dibb Lupton Alsop	563	London	+44 171 248 4141
Herbert Smith	553	London	+44 171 374 8000
Nabarro Nathanson	502	London	+44 171 493 9933
Norton Rose	475	London	+44 171 283 6000
Hammond Suddards	404	Leeds	+44 113 284 7000
Denton Hall	377	London	+44 171 242 1212
Ashurst Morris Crisp	334	London	+44 171 638 1111
Shoosmiths & Harrison	326	Northampton	+44 1604 29977
Cameron McKenna	323	London	+44 171 367 3000
Wilde Sapte	320	London	+44 171 246 7000
Pinsent Curtis	305	Birmingham	+44 121 200 1050
Irwin Mitchell	288	Sheffield	+44 114 276 7777
Richards Butler	283	London	+44 171 247 6555
Clyde & Co	275	London	+44 171 623 1244
Edge & Ellison	267	Birmingham	+44 121 200 2001
Booth & Co	258	Leeds	+44 113 283 2000
Masons	258	London	+44 171 490 4000
Stephenson Harwood	250	London	+44 171 329 4422
Davies Arnold Cooper	242	London	+44 171 936 2222
Wansbroughs Willey Hargrave	236	Bristol	+44 117 926 8981
Thompsons	234	London	+44 171 637 9761
Wragge & Co	231	Birmingham	+44 121 233 1000

EU (excluding UK)

	No. of lawyers	City	Telephone
Fidal	1,024	Paris	+33 1 46394646
Nauta Dutilh	300	Amsterdam	+31 20 5414646
De Brauw Blackstone Westbroek	274	Amsterdam	+31 20 5771771
Loeff Claeys Verbeke	240	Amsterdam	+31 20 5741200
Archibald Andersen Association d'Avocats	220	Paris	+33 1 42910700
Oppenhoff & Rädler	216	Berlin	+49 30 214960
Trenité Van Doorne	210	Amsterdam	+31 20 6789123
Gide Loyrette Nouel	204	Paris	+33 1 40756000
HSD Ernst & Young	204	Paris	+33 1 46937000
Loyens & Volkmaars	189	Amsterdam	+31 20 5785785

USA

	No. of lawyers	City	Telephone
Baker & McKenzie	1,776	New York	+1 212 751 5700
Jones, Day, Reavis & Pogue	1,014	New York	+1 212 326 3939
Skadden, Arps, Slate Meagher & Flom	1,001	New York	+1 212 735 3000
Morgan, Lewis and Bockius	732	New York	+1 212 309 6000
Mayer, Brown & Platt	639	New York	+1 212 554 3000
Fulbright & Jaworksi	615	New York	+1 212 489 1033
Sidley & Austin	607	New York	+1 212 906 2000
Latham & Watkins	575	New York	+1 212 906 1200
Weil, Gotshal & Manges	575	New York	+1 212 310 8000
White and Case	554	New York	+1 212 819 8200

Sources: Legalese (UK and EU); American Lawyer (USA).

Note: Data are for 1996.